Nature Spirits

Nature Spirits and What they Say

Interviews with Verena Staël von Holstein

Edited by Wolfgang Weirauch

Floris Books

Translated by Brian Strevens

First published in German under the title
Was die Naturgeister uns sagen
by Flensburger Hefte Verlag, Flensburg, 2001
First published in English in 2004 by Floris Books
Reprinted 2005

British Library CIP Data available

ISBN 0-86315-462-X

Printed in Great Britain
By Bell & Bain Ltd, Glasgow

Contents

Foreword

Wolfgang Weirauch

In late summer 2001, shortly before the world was shaken by the attacks in New York of September 11, a manuscript from Verena Staël von Holstein arrived in our office, entitled *Conversations with Miller*. It appeared that, between March 1, 2000 and February 28, 2001, she and her husband, Friedrich Pfannenschmidt, had held conversations with nature spirits. Now it was lying there, her book proposal, five hundred A4 pages — far too much text for a normal publication.

For almost a year we didn't touch the manuscript. But then, in the summer of 2002, I got to work on the text, recognized the value of these conversations and arranged to meet the writer, along with her husband. I still had doubts, I must admit. What would be waiting for me? Some kind of medium? Somebody on a huge ego trip? A dramatic spectacle?

In fact, after reading through the manuscript, most of my doubts had already disappeared, and my very last concerns vanished when I came to know the individuals and the nature spirits themselves.

They live in a watermill among scenic surroundings by a river in the Lüneburger Heide, a heathland region in Northern Germany. I visited them three times, and over a period of four days spoke myself with the nature spirits — and those meetings were extraordinary!

I discovered that Verena Staël von Holstein had learnt over many years to work on her supersensory perceptions so that she is able to translate almost simultaneously the language of the elemental beings into our human terms. And so the interviews took place with seventeen nature spirits, almost as though seventeen human beings were sitting in front of me.

As the interviews began, I allowed the nature spirits to penetrate all my thoughts and then, speaking aloud, I asked the first of the beings my questions. Verena Staël von Holstein received the answers spiritually in the form of patterns, ideas and sometimes also images, and conveyed the answers vocally. And they all spoke differently, some going into details, many just giving very brief answers, so that often I had to ask again to get a satisfactory reply. Now and again I was refused an answer or it was bluntly explained to me that my question was nonsensical, and once in a while I had to hold playful little battles of words with the nature spirits, just to get one more answer. The answers mostly came in a flash, and now and again the answer came even before I had properly put the question. They had read my thoughts!

Unfortunately no exact names exist for these beings. Here we use the following terms synonymously: elemental being, elemental spirit, nature-being, nature spirit and also spirit being. In a more precise sense the four elements are represented by the elemental beings — the Stone One, the Sandy One, the Watery One, the Airy One and the Fiery One. The Little Glass Man, the Paper Being, the Salt Child or the Silver One are not elemental beings in the same sense, but represent spheres of nature and are without any difficulty to be described as nature-beings. In the case of the two house spirits — Miller and Quadrom — the definition becomes more difficult. They are active only partly in the elemental sphere, only partially in nature, but predominantly in the house. On the other hand all animal, marsh, plant and tree beings are clearly nature spirits, but not elemental beings.

Nonetheless all beings are active somewhere in nature, consequently they are nature spirits. They're also active in the etheric-spirit elemental particles or forces out of which our world is composed, and in this respect they're also elemental beings. Only the High One, a higher being, who speaks in the spirit of Michael, doesn't belong to this category.

The different ways of speaking of the seventeen beings are difficult to convey. The conversations were often amusing and surprising, from time to time very serious, and often simply beautiful. One clearly experienced the atmosphere intensifying as the High One spoke. The Stone One was also impressive, speaking in a peculiar grammatical tense which doesn't exist for us, but which is intended to express his state of permanence — past, present and future rolled into one.

The nature spirits have no human morality, but they know exactly how they can hurt and how they can help humans. They live in the spiritual-etheric interconnections of nature, they hold the world together and ensure the continued existence of the earth. They have never known freedom in the way that humans know it. Some of them are friends with one another, but what love is or how the feeling of love is experienced, they have also never known. They perceive the supersensible world, but how it is to live in a dark prison, in a physical body, and not to perceive the supersensible world is completely unknown to them.

In order to experience more closely this new land — morality, love, freedom, ignorance of the spiritual world — seventeen spirit beings have set out as a kind of advance party in order to speak with human beings. These conversations are extraordinarily important for them, because up to now the angels were their rulers, and taught them their tasks. But the angels are now withdrawing and leaving the elemental beings more and more alone. Human beings are their new masters, but human beings know nothing about them. For this reason the nature spirits are suffering and are afraid of humans. That's precisely why these conversations between human beings and nature spirits are so important, for both sides. Both partners can learn from one another, draw closer to one another and cooperate in a totally new way.

When you read these conversations you will be able to immerse yourself into the world of the elemental beings, into the different spheres of responsibility of each being. You will experience many things which are new, but also things which are well-known, as well as secrets of the past and the future.

It may be that mistakes have occurred in the process of

transmission, but to the best of our ability we have sought to avoid this. The texts were edited, given to Verena Staël von Holstein and Friedrich Pfannenschmidt and also read aloud to the nature spirits. Taking all this into account I can vouch for the authenticity of the contents.

We know that humans speaking to elemental beings is nothing new. In ancient times that was common practice, and even today there are isolated individuals with such abilities. What is new here is the approach of elemental beings to humans because they have a longing to speak with them, because they would like to learn from them, speak about themselves, work together with humans in the future in many projects and would like to ask them questions.

The way of contact which Verena Staël von Holstein has with nature spirits is also new, together with their wish to disseminate the conversations through the medium of print. This contact is not mediumistic, in other words it does not occur in a state of changed consciousness, and has not come about through any particular path of inner training. Verena Staël von Holstein is an anthroposophist, one who sets out to follow the spiritual indications of Rudolf Steiner, but her ability to perceive etheric and astral spheres of human beings and nature is something she has possessed since she was a child. She has so trained this ability over years through arduous work that communication with the nature spirits takes place almost without difficulty.

The content of the conversations stands and speaks for itself. Allow yourself to be enchanted by the world of the nature spirits. But recognize also the seriousness of the situation. We humans owe the elemental beings so much, and that is why we should practise a completely new approach to them. In this book you will find how that may be done.

Preliminary Remarks

Verena Staël von Holstein and the nature spirits

The spirit beings and the people involved in the creation of this book do *not* see it as their task to help other people deal with their own lives. Therefore no recipes for happiness are going to be handed out nor any questions answered about past, present or future incarnations of individual persons.

It is much more the urgent wish of the spirit beings with the help of the people here to awaken the general consciousness of the people of this culture to the fact that our Earth is a living being. It is inhabited by humans, animals, plants, minerals and spirit beings.

At present this living Earth-being faces the danger of being destroyed by its human inhabitants. To avert this danger people have to turn again to facts which are not to be found in the physical world but in the spiritual world. The contents of this book aim to help towards this.

There are many people who entertain doubts with regard to the content and the creation of this book and who, for example, want proofs for the existence of the spirit beings or for the truthfulness of the persons involved.

To these people it may be said that such proof is unnecessary or rather, not at all possible. Something that is not part of the physical world cannot be proven within the physical world. Nowadays it is left to each individual as to whether or not they can view the existence of the spiritual world as a fact, or believe in the ability of an individual to perceive spiritually.

Those people who only recognize physical proofs are recommended to read Antoine de Saint-Exupéry's book *The Little Prince*, where the fox says to the little prince, "One only sees clearly with the heart. The essence is invisible to the eyes!" (Chapter 21).

Verena Staël von Holstein

Living with Nature Spirits

An interview with Verena Staël von Holstein

Wolfgang Weirauch: When did you consciously see nature spirits for the first time?

Verena Staël von Holstein: I can't answer that exactly, because they were always there. It must have been a slow process connected to the dawning of my childhood awareness. They were always around me; in certain periods they appeared more clearly than at others. They appeared very clearly from the age of nine to twelve, when I attended the Waldorf School in Benefeld. During this time I often went to a little birch wood, where I played with the nature spirits.

WW: And this contact with them was something completely normal?

VS: Yes, it was normal and everyday. I didn't give much thought to my special abilities and didn't speak to other people about them. I don't know exactly when the perception of the elemental beings began, possibly between two and three years old, when I was still living in Rendsburg. I can remember a large railway embankment there where I saw various beings of whom I was afraid.

WW: Have you always seen the beings or only on particular days or else when you were in natural surroundings?

VS: Always.

WW: Indoors as well?

VS: Not so clearly. The first ones, as I mentioned, were the beings by the railway, then the beings in the birches. Birch beings are girls, or rather women, when the birches are old. There were beings in the house in Benefeld, especially in the cellar, but they didn't play such a big role in my life. The essence of the house spirit has only become apparent to me here in the watermill through our house spirit, Miller.

WW: When did you first speak to people about your seeing things that others don't see?

VS: I always knew what I was seeing. My parents and my grandmother were quite open to this sphere of experience. My grandmother, who was born in 1886, also had contact with nature-beings — though more unconsciously, she perceived them in a very dreamy way. She was not a "head" person. She was small and tubby and a wonderful grandmother and she told us a wealth of stories about different nature spirits. It was especially after my grandfather died that she had a lot of time for me and conveyed to me in a playful manner a lot about invisible beings.

WW: At that time, did you already refer to the nature-beings with clear names or terms?

VS: No, that I started here in the watermill. I could differentiate them, but not with the clarity I have today. In the meantime, I've come to understand that these beings have their own personalities.

WW: Have you ever had times when you didn't see these beings?

VS: No, but I didn't always pay much attention to them. I've always seen them, but later on they were no longer in the forefront. I then went to university and through my profession spent much time at sea — I sailed on a research ship as hydrographic engineer on the North Sea and the Atlantic — there I perceived the nature-beings more clearly again. Later, I earned my living as a computer programmer, working in surroundings where nature-beings have scarcely any importance.

WW: Does the perception of nature-beings disappear when working with a PC and the internet?

VS: Not with me, though it does slip on to another level. It's like childhood memories; one isn't always thinking about them, but they are present nevertheless. I could pick up contact with the nature-beings again and again, and especially when I was feeling down, I used to seek contact, for example, with tree beings.

But that's not so easy. You can't just go up and lean against a tree and expect something from the tree spirits or other nature spirits. It's not so simple. The spirit beings have to get to know you first.

WW: When did you come here, to the watermill, and how did the resident spirit beings make contact with you?

VS: The contact with the beings came back quite clearly eight years ago during my pregnancy. A dramatic change took place when I was pregnant. My parents-in-law lived here in the watermill, which was in desperate need of renovation. Though it was never openly expressed, my father-in-law had always been waiting for his son to have an heir. The moment he knew that I was pregnant he let go and died within three months.

My mother-in-law couldn't cope with the property and the animals by herself, so my husband asked me if I would like to move with him here to the mill. So, heavily pregnant, I moved in. About two months later my daughter was born, and shortly after that I came into closer contact with the resident beings. Suddenly I felt a presence, which wanted something from me. That was Miller, the house spirit. And he confirmed to me that the beings of decay, who shortly before were still present in this watermill, had now moved out.

WW: Did you see these beings of decay when you moved in?

VS: Yes.

WW: What did they look like?

VS: Grey. Like spiders' webs, not so much like clouds of mist but more like physical spiders' webs. If you look etherically at spiders however, they shine like a prism. They are very colourful and fascinating to look at. That's probably the reason why so many people are afraid of spiders.

WW: Why?

VS: People experience the etheric when observing a spider, even if they cannot consciously perceive it.

WW: But isn't a shining prism something beautiful?

VS: Of course. But one can also be afraid of intense beauty. But that's just a hunch of mine.

WW: Did the first contact with the house spirit take place when you mentioned that you had noticed that the beings of decay had left the mill?

VS: Yes. When I asked him his name, he said, "Miller." Only about two years later did I realize the connection between his name Miller and this mill. It wasn't at all clear to me in the first two years. Sometimes you just don't see things that are right in front of your nose.

WW: What then did Miller say at the beginning, and then what did the other beings, who came one after the other, say to you at first?

VS: At first they asked, "What sort of a person are you? Can you let us come close to you?" They look at you and they saw, for example, that I love my husband. At the beginning of our relationship it was very important for Miller to comprehend how the change in ownership of this mill took place; that after the death of my father-in-law, my husband and I took over the running of this house. The relationship to my mother-in-law was also important for Miller, for just like my husband, he experienced quite a drama with her. She had no relationship at all to nature-beings or the supernatural. My mother-in-law had burdened this house with her attitude, and Miller had to get this off his chest. He had to learn to formulate it as much as possible in human terms. In that way, he could then understand it better.

The improvement in the understanding between humans and nature spirits was the first thing that happened between us. You then search for a common language. He asks, "What do you mean when you say, 'wood'?" That's a simple example. And then when you answer him, he says that he calls the same thing 'wood' as well. It's more difficult with terms that are strongly connected to humans, such as, "What is 'soul'? Show me what you call 'soul'." Or, "Show me what you call 'beautiful'." We then have to demonstrate it to them, but that's a huge job. This is done by imagining these terms as vividly as possible.

WW: Do please describe how you communicate with the nature-beings.

VS: At the beginning, I saw the nature spirits as concretely as in a photograph, and I drew them as well. And then I simply spoke quite normally to them. Words spoken out loud are very important to them. Though it doesn't have to be like that when speaking to the nature spirits. But the spoken word has a special meaning for them, because every word changes the world. The word is a reality.

We moved here into the mill in August 1995. In the course of the years our level of communication has changed. Now I perceive the nature spirits for example, by noticing exactly where Miller is, even if I can't see him. I feel the presence of these beings. And then I communicate with these beings using patterns. Pattern is the most appropriate expression. When Miller is concerned about something and wants to inform my husband that somewhere in the mill something has to be repaired, he sends me a kind of pattern and I must translate it into German. These beings don't speak German, even though their language is connected to this region.

WW: Are they just patterns or also images? Are they put into words or does the understanding or the knowledge of what the nature-beings are saying come almost automatically into your thinking?

VS: They aren't images, rather words and patterns. It's more than a bare term, it's like a connection of patterns. It can maybe be compared to a three-dimensional model of the atom. That's roughly how one can imagine what these beings say.

WW: But how do you get these patterns into the words of the German language?

VS: That's the problem!

WW: Rudolf Steiner said something similar. His great accomplishment as researcher of the spirit world may not have been so much the investigation of those regions, but rather putting into words what he saw.

VS: My husband helps me a lot with this translation. I stutter and stammer around, then my husband formulates it and I say that it still isn't quite correct. Then he often chooses a new formulation and I say where the sticking points are. This goes on until we've found the right words and terms. By the way, if you're tired, the contact with these beings is easier than when you're mentally alert.

WW: Is that because the intellect is a kind of barrier to these beings?

VS: Yes, the intellect gets in the way for most people. Now, however, the conversations with the nature spirits are a lot more proficient, and I can mostly conduct a dialogue with them as fast as I can now with you.

WW: After first asking your questions and conversing out loud, did afterwards a phase come in which the beings could also read your thoughts?

VS: Yes, I gave them my permission.

WW: Do you have to think about a question intensively and word for word for the beings to understand it?

VS: When it's something very important, then it should be spoken out loud. If, for example, you're being pestered by a being, you should say quite loud and clear, "Go away!" With things that aren't so important, everyday matters arising through contact with these beings, it's enough to talk to them in thoughts when you know them well. You should think as much as possible in words, because there's a difference between simply letting a thought pass through your awareness or thinking intensively in words. The thought must embody itself in the word.

WW: And they don't perceive the teeming bustle of thoughts and inner life in this way?

VS: That gets on their nerves. We chose the term word-junk for it.

WW: Are there any rules governing the contact between humans and spirit beings?

VS: We're working on these at the moment. You should be honest. Lies devour the soul. You should try to look on the nature spirits as personalities, even if they don't have a self in the same way as humans. You should realize that even in small things there is something of a personality. But the most important thing is honesty in dealing with one another. Some of them place value on manners; that you're polite and say, for example, "Thank you," and "Please." But that's not the case with all of them.

WW: In other words, it matters that you greet them and thank them when they talk to you, and that you say goodbye?

VS: Yes, they like that a lot, especially when this takes on a kind of rhythm. For our book I performed this kind of formal ceremony, but not in everyday dealings. Though when the High One comes, his appearing is itself a kind of ceremony.

WW: Are nature spirits allowed to simply read the thoughts of humans?

VS: Not just like that. Firstly, it's taboo and they require the permission of a person for as long as the thought belongs to him and is still connected to his feelings. But when the thought is freed from the person and has entered the impersonal thought sphere, then of course they may read it. Humans are free and nature spirits are not allowed to simply intrude into the freedom of humans. For this reason, the person has to say "yes" to these beings "passing through him." Humans have to agree to allow the nature spirits to read their thoughts and the emotional dynamic belonging to them.

WW: But does a person have any idea what he's letting himself in for giving such permission.

VS: Probably not. But it's anyway not a normal human practice and I've only ever carried it out with two or three people. Not everyone that visits us has to allow these beings to pass through him. You're only the third one.

WW: That means therefore, that for this interview all the nature spirits present are reading my thoughts and even know my questions just by my thinking them?

VS: Yes, and they know your feelings as well.

WW: When you're reading a book, do the beings read with you?

VS: Normally not.

WW: Aren't they interested, or why not?

VS: When we're reading something by Rudolf Steiner they listen. When I read science fiction novels, at most they'll briefly look over my shoulder and start to giggle. They're not interested in them.

WW: Can you arrange the nature spirits into groups a little? Do the beings themselves have definite criteria for telling themselves apart and according to which they're organized?

VS: The beings are quite clearly hierarchically organized. A house being like Miller is the head of all the house beings in this house. He is the head of the hierarchy and then he has his subordinates. These are beings who are subject to him, and in fact in such a crude way, as was the case in human society in the distant past. They have to do what Miller instructs them to do. And the lower the level in the hierarchy the house beings are, the more insignificant their work. The beings become more and more atomlike. And Miller is the top of the pyramid of house beings.

It's similar with the Green Ones, the plant beings. Here there is a hierarchy of plant spirits, starting at the bottom with the really small plant beings who fulfil the smallest, single tasks in the plant. The being of a single plant works, for example, on a higher level of the hierarchy. An even higher being then, is Gnunno, who has to take care of a whole region, but only the plants, except for the trees, because trees form a special group. Gnunno forms the region's canopy, he protects the plants in this region. And then there's another being who forms the connection to the plant-self, reaching up therefore into the highest spiritual regions, presumably up into the so-called Higher Devachan.

Every sphere in nature, every plant, the sand, every river, the wind has this hierarchy and every being occupies a definite level in the hierarchy.

WW: How many beings, for example, belong to the hierarchy of this house?

VS: Sixteen thousand, seven hundred and forty-three — that's what Miller's just told me. But that's leaving the really small ones out. With them you can't really speak anymore of personality. Some are responsible for the doors, others for the chairs and again others for the supply of warmth.

WW: Are house spirits elemental beings?

A stable on Miller´s estate

VS: No, they form their own group. The elemental beings belong to the four elements — mineral, water, air, fire. House beings are very similar to human beings and at the same time they're close to the gnomes. They can be compared to humans. On the other hand, when you approach a fire being that's a completely different kind of being. Fire beings also have a hierarchy — on a small scale the being of a candle-flame and on a large scale the being of a house fire or even of a volcano.

In the case of water there are the tiny water children and then for example, there's the nix who's responsible for a very large region. Here we have a nix, Echevit, the Watery One, who has his focus in our house but who's actually a nix of the River Elbe. He's a spirit active on a higher level whose sphere of activity extends now and again to the North Sea. He also has his countless helpers. In the case of the stone beings it's similar, but here you have to differentiate again between sand and stone beings. Sand actually consists of small stones, nevertheless sand is something different from a large stone.

WW: What's it like with the air beings?

VS: Exactly the same. There are the small movements of air and the beings responsible for them and then for example, there's a storm. Air and wind beings are actually different beings. Valliniyu, who is with us here, is responsible for the sphere of air and light in this region. The wind itself moves through this air and light sphere. The west wind comes from the Atlantic, where it's born, and dies down over Russia. *What did you say, Valliniyu?*

The Airy One: It's born again, becomes a strong wind, and then the structures in the strong wind become weaker until they slowly disintegrate and turn into smaller structures. It's like a mesh, in which the single pieces become starting-points for a new mesh. In between it breaks up. The wind beings travel with the wind, but don't die when the wind dies down, they just simply change.

WW: Can you apply the categories of good and evil to these beings?

VS: No, in this context these categories are absurd. The beings of decay for example are necessary. A decaying animal corpse in nature is certainly no lovely sight for humans, but it's a necessity. Nature spirits don't distinguish between good and evil in our sense. They actually distinguish six categories:

— beings who are helpful towards humans
— beings who are harmful towards humans
— beings who are committed to growth
— beings who are committed to decay
— beings entrusted with protection
— beings entrusted with destruction

WW: In describing the opposing powers, anthroposophy speaks about spectres and demons or simply evil. From the point of view of those nature spirits present here, demons aren't evil beings?

VS: These are beings who in general are connected to a descending development, while the beings present here are connected to an ascending development. The nature spirits definitely experience the beings at the head of the descending development as a kind of threat. Miller for example, is scared stiff of the higher, darker beings. Fear also exists for these beings. House spirits are also subject to attacks, which Miller isn't able to withstand. So he has to get together with other beings, and in this respect it's good that different beings have their focus here in the watermill. Here we have the rare phenomenon that in the room in the mill which you've just seen, the weir room, there's a kind of communal focus for many nature spirits.

WW: Can you apply the categories masculine and feminine in respect of nature spirits?

VS: Yes, especially in the sphere of the animal beings, because there are masculine and feminine animals. These are of course human categories. Nature spirits can at best be described as being more masculine or more feminine. It's not so black and white as with us.

WW: What then is masculine and feminine in Nature?

VS: It's the expression or rather the spiritual impression, which corresponds more to a woman or to a man. Miller can sometimes also be very feminine. The Brown One on the other hand is very masculine. You really feel that he's masculine, with a beard and everything that goes with it. On the other hand, for elemental beings, sand beings for example, it's completely absurd to speak of masculine and feminine beings. You anyway have to bear in mind with these categories that they're people's projections and don't come from these beings.

WW: When you perceive one of these beings, couldn't it be that you're projecting the form of this being? In other words, when you see the Brown One in the form of a man with a beard, in the form of a shepherd, couldn't it be that this is just your subjective projection and another person would see him completely differently?

VS: Obviously every person would see these beings differently, but not completely differently. The Brown One would certainly be seen by everyone as a masculine being. Certain basic structures remain similar, others would be seen differently through the subjectivity of the person. The beings reflect the pictures that stream towards them from humans.

The beings also have their own humour. Echevit, the Nix, for example, can be quite a laugh. He disguises himself. And he does it because he enjoys it. He can appear sometimes in one form and sometimes another.

WW: Does Echevit actually know that his name is the same, at least according to how it's pronounced, as that of the current Turkish president.

VS: Yes, he does. Though his real name is untranslatable and very much longer. Echevit is a kind of summary of this longer name.

WW: How do the spirit beings communicate with one another?

VS: That's a good question, and I can't answer it exactly for all beings. I don't fully understand these connections. Some beings, such as Miller and Echevit sit next to one another and simply communicate with one another. But a fire being, for example, doesn't sit down next to other nature spirits, but appears in another form. How it communicates with other beings is very hard for me to picture.

At the same time, the term "layer," referred to before as a sphere of thought (see page 19), always comes to mind, in the sense of a layer around the earth. An etheric-spiritual layer exists, which is like a thin cloth draped around the earth and permeating it in a form which cannot be described in mathematical terms. The knowledge of the world is contained in this layer. All the thoughts and actions of humans are also stored here. And when the beings want to, they meet in this layer and communicate with one another. This layer embraces the whole earth, perhaps corresponding to the Akashic Chronicle described in detail by Steiner.

WW: While you're speaking to me are you also simultaneously hearing several of these beings speaking to you? That what these beings are saying consequently merges seamlessly with you?

VS: Yes, it's like a conversation between humans. There are sometimes also problems of understanding. These mostly come up when it's to do with human themes, because for many of these the nature spirits have no terms.

WW: What kind of humour do the elemental beings have?

VS: They have a lot of humour and are always in the mood for a joke, but this humour doesn't always correspond to human morality. For example, they find it funny when a milk jug falls on someone's foot. We ourselves don't find it all that funny, but the nature spirits will laugh themselves silly over it.

WW: How do the nature spirits laugh? What does it sound like?

VS: A bit like a clear-sounding bell, very lovely.

WW: Do all beings have this kind of humour, or is it mainly the gnomes?

VS: It's mainly Miller, whereas the Watery One has fun disguising himself. Flame beings can really laugh. When a fire spirit really feels so good that it laughs through a flame then it's almost possible to see it with physical eyes. When the air is content it blows like a gentle breeze. The Brown One has a relatively coarse sense of humour. And the joy of the High One is simply indescribable. It's as if the world were laughing. When the High One laughs, one is simply happy.

WW: Do nature spirits have a kind of morality?

VS: No, not at all. This is something they want to learn from humans. Why do humans have a sense of morality, what do they hope to achieve with it? They say that all our machines which we manufacture here on the earth will appear as nature-beings in the next planetary incarnation of the earth. They can perceive in that something like a moral connection.

WW: I know of this connection from Rudolf Steiner.

VS: Did he describe it as well? I didn't know that.

WW: He said something like, everything that now belongs to the world of machines will become the basis for existence on Jupiter — as Steiner calls the next stage of development of the earth. However, this basis will no longer be a physical-material one.

VS: The nature-beings say that as well, and that's why they demand from us that we construct all machines in a beautiful way.

WW: Steiner also speaks about all the merely intellectual thoughts with which we understand just the dense material world, all the shadow-like automatic thoughts which we don't fill with spiritual life, suddenly turning into spider-like beings in the eighth millennium.* These automaton-like spider-beings will be of a mineral-plant nature, and gifted with an intense power of reason, but also be terrifyingly evil. And in their worldwide webs all those humans will get entangled who haven't raised themselves to the spirit. But that's in a distant future. Though it makes you realize clearly what responsibility a person has for all his thoughts and deeds.

VS: The High One especially emphasizes this, but Echevit, the Watery One, speaks about it too. Until about the fifteenth century he was a kind of local god here, a Nix, who was worshipped by humans. People of past ages knew that a Nix lived here and so they brought him small offerings.

WW: Were these offerings made at definite times of the year or on definite occasions?

VS: The offerings were made, for example, before the summer floods which have always occurred here and at Christmas, at the winter solstice, with the plea that the Nix stay here.

WW: Why should the Nix stay here in Winter?

VS: At that time people assumed the Nixes didn't have to return when they undertook their regular journeys. *Do they have to return, Echevit?*

The Watery One: We don't have any freedom. The bonds tying us to the location are tightening more and more as the earth ages. In the past the water-beings could leave for good when the circumstances called for it. Now they can't do that anymore. The older the earth becomes, the more important becomes the point on the earth where we have our home and our tasks.

* See Rudolf Steiner, *Materialism and the Task of Anthroposophy,* Rudolf Steiner Press, London & Anthroposophic Press, New York 1987. Lecture of May 13, 1921, p. 263.

WW: How did your book project come about? Who had the idea?

VS: All of us together. The nature spirits kept on mentioning that they actually wanted to reach more people. They asked how this might be possible. We then had a kind of brainstorming session. One possibility would have been to get people to come here, but my husband was not too keen on that. Then I read in a magazine of a woman who had painted an angel every day. In the process this woman had many experiences. I was very moved by that.

As a result the nature spirits asked me whether we couldn't do something similar and hold a conversation every day. They were hoping to achieve a multi-layered effect. For one thing their thoughts would get further out into the world. For another I would learn to meditate correctly and to nurture the contact with the nature spirits. Furthermore, we would all be developing something that was in tune with the spirit of the age. And so we decided on this book project which we submitted to you. We began on March 1, 2000.

WW: How exactly did you proceed? Did you hold similar conversations to the ones we're holding now? Did your husband write the conversations down?

VS: At first we wanted to record the conversations with a dictaphone and my husband intended to edit them afterwards for style. For various reasons this turned out not to be feasible. I didn't know how to handle the machine properly and I wasn't satisfied with the situation. So we acquired a speech recognition programme, software with which you can dictate directly into the computer.

And after I'd got used to the speech recognition programme, I could simply dictate my thoughts and the dialogues with the nature-beings. Afterwards my husband edited them. This had the advantage that I immediately saw on screen what I'd been saying. With a dictaphone you don't see what you've said, indeed you can't even be sure that it's actually recording. That's why you should now and again check if your dictaphone is really recording, because what we're doing here at the moment is not altogether being looked upon with favour.

WW: Who isn't looking favourably at our undertaking?

VS: The forces of evil. They don't want any sort of information about the spiritual world to reach human awareness, because humans who are ignorant are far easier to control than those who aren't. The nature spirits taking part in our project want to pass on this information. And above all they want to get to know their new masters. The hierarchies of the angels are withdrawing from guiding humans, also from directly influencing the elemental beings. They're handing over the shaping of the earth's future more and more to humans.

WW: And humans don't understand the nature spirits!

VS: Exactly. Humans don't make any effort to understand the nature spirits. For the most part they don't even know they exist.

WW: That must be terrible for these beings.

VS: It's dreadful! Some of them are in complete despair. When you see an elemental being in despair you become terribly sad. Sometimes I even cry.

Next door we have the marsh. The "One from the Marsh" rules there. Nature-beings from Hamburg, such as tree beings, come to him. They come here as sick, tired, exhausted and despairing elemental beings. And that's because humans don't notice them and humans don't cultivate any contact with them. This blindness in human behaviour is in accordance with the intentions of the forces of evil, especially the Ahrimanic beings. When the human being is blind to the connection with the elemental beings, it's then possible for Ahrimanic beings to act at this point.

That's why the nature spirits' most pressing concern is to make their new rulers aware. Humans should know about the nature spirits and their influence, and they should become aware of what they themselves do. After all humans are continually generating nature-beings through all their actions, thoughts and feelings. When humans have to tamper with plants and trees or when they build houses, they're continually generating through their actions all sorts of nature-beings. And these can be positive or negative beings.

WW: But it's the human being who decides what happens. Or is it possible for the Ahrimanic beings to stop our project — the book as well as this interview — when we want to carry it through?

VS: A lot has been done so that the project will fail to materialize. Aimed at you and us. At the moment we're sitting under a silver dome, which is our personal protective shield. The Silver Being has spun this shield. In addition we have the tone E flat as a bell over us. And finally the High One is present to protect us. And in order to defeat him a much higher spirit from the other side has to come.

WW: What has happened in particular to prevent this project from materializing?

VS: Many things one after another, but about which I don't want to speak at the moment.

WW: From a certain moment on in your manuscript, the nature spirits begin to ask you and your husband questions. I take it that they have an enormous interest in experiencing things about humans which they themselves don't comprehend.

VS: First they asked if they might put questions to us. They enquired as well, if they could be present for all the things happening in the house, because everything that humans do interests them. They're interested in why humans brush their teeth, they're also interested in why humans go to the toilet. Nature spirits don't go to the toilet. They're also interested in why we speak into peculiar gadgets which record our voices in order to preserve the words. And then they suggest, if it wouldn't be a lot easier to do it by means of the "layer" which they use to communicate.

Then they're interested in what love is. And it's not easy to answer when you get asked such a profound question. They also ask quite concrete questions, such as, why a road has been built here or there. Mostly they have matters of concern connected with these events. "Can't you tell the humans they shouldn't undertake any building projects at this location?" But in the meantime they've realized that we as ordinary people don't have any influence over these things. It was relatively arduous explaining to them that such a project can't simply be stopped because, for example, it annoys a mountain spirit.

WW: That's possible in Iceland.

VS: Yes, that's true. There the people deal with elemental beings, the so-called "little people," in such a natural way. Sometimes they also want to have tips how they could prevent such projects. But they also address things which lie beyond any human comprehension, such as: "Do you really know what effect it has when you send a space probe to Mars?" Of course at first nothing occurrs to us. And then they challenge us to find out something in order to speak to them about it later.

WW: Each side in the conversation refers to a diversity of things beyond the other one's sphere of life, whose otherness they only comprehend gradually. Here you surely quite often come up against limiting factors.

VS: You come up against quite definite limiting factors, particularly limits of understanding. You can't explain certain things to a fire being at all, because they're not in tune with its nature. In such cases the beings say nothing, perhaps out of politeness, even though they don't understand it.

WW: Such politeness exists?

VS: Yes, absolutely. If I want to explain to a fire being that it hurts me when it comes too near to me, or when I touch a flame, it can acknowledge this fact, but it doesn't understand it, because it wants to be nice to me by touching me. In this respect these beings often have something very childlike about them. That fire hurts is incomprehensible for a fire being. For a fire being, fire is spirit.

WW: What do the nature spirits most fail to understand about humans?

VS: Mainly freedom and everything connected to it. It's the same with love. They ask about the difference between nature spirits and humans, they want to know exactly what makes humans human. And they're insistent that humans and nature spirits should travel the path into the future better together. They know that something totally new is approaching humans.

WW: Can they also look into the future?

VS: The High One can, and Echevit as well. But they can only do so within certain limits, for the future is open. Humans shape the future.

WW: But not certain things.

VS: Here it gets more difficult. In the same way that the details have an effect on the whole, so the whole also has an effect on the details. Time is a phenomenon which has to do with humans. The nature-beings stand outside of time. Kapuvu, the Stone One, expresses this most clearly. He speaks in a very strange grammatical tense, with which he's roughly expressing that everything has already happened a long time ago, even if it's still lying in the future. Humans, nevertheless, can shape the future. They can even change the past.

WW: How do you change the past?

VS: By being alive and shaping the future. If you really want to understand this, then you have to meditate very intensively, culminating in the painful experience that you have to call human consciousness into question. For the human being only experiences himself in space and time. He has an object-based and limited awareness, with which he experiences a selective, earthly present. But nature spirits don't live in time. They live in a continuous spiritual present, and this is open to the eternal. If you want to picture that concretely, it's difficult. Past, present and future always remain in balance, and when humans undertake something in the world, they change the future as well as the past for the nature spirits. When you understand that, you get a feeling for time and eternity.

WW: What concerns me especially is the already mentioned dividing wall between present-day mankind and the nature spirits, above all the despair of the nature spirits over humans no longer perceiving them. Could you describe that a little more graphically, so that the readers could understand what responsibility we humans carry?

VS: We couldn't exist at all without the nature spirits. The entire earth would perish without their working. They're tirelessly creating in the forces of growth and decay in nature — in the smallest plant as well as in the wider climatic relationships. The nature-beings are integrated into the total, wisdom-filled connections of nature. And so that they could act in accordance with this wisdom, an angel or a being from a higher hierarchy, was always standing at the head of their hierarchy instructing and leading them to some extent. They acted in accordance with this higher wisdom.

Today however, the angels' responsibility is step by step shifting to humans. Humans are responsible for nature, they have to look after the earth and nature. And they're responsible for their own thoughts, feelings and deeds, with which they're constantly producing new beings. But mankind can only fulfil this responsibility if they work together with the nature spirits, if they know about them and their tasks. And the nature spirits need this cooperation so that they can accomplish their tasks for the benefit of the earth and mankind.

The present situation of the nature spirits can be compared to the work in a firm without a competent director at the head. Because the new management isn't aware of its task, it becomes even harder for the nature spirits to perform their tasks, for they are actually so structured that they want to be instructed. The nature spirits would like to know for sure if what they're doing is also right. They would like to know if their creative work is still able to sustain this world. And then the nature spirits come and ask, "Am I doing it right, boss?" But the boss doesn't even know they exist.

So it would be nice if human beings gradually became more sensitive to certain perceptions. Then they'd notice they were being nudged now and again by the nature spirits, so that they become aware of them. Humans should wake up, reconsider their lives and change their relationship to nature and the nature spirits. Now and again people experience such situations, which are tantamount to an alarm call. They could also be caused by angels. Humans only have to pay attention, otherwise the call will go unheeded.

I have a good friend, who works as a forester, who sometimes has the feeling when he's standing in front of a tree, that someone is watching him. This is an initial contact between humans and nature-beings, which is taking place on an more unconscious level. There are even people with "green fingers," who act in close communion with these beings even when they know nothing about them. But most people are totally blind to the nature-beings, their actions and our connection to them. And that has to change.

Nature Spirits

Interviewed by Wolfgang Weirauch
through the mediation of
Verena Staël von Holstein

The Nature-beings

The High One: member of the hierarchies, connected to humans and their freedom, guardian of the good powers.

Kapuvu, the Stone One: connected to stone, guardian of the ground of the region.

Echevit, the Watery One: a Nix, connected to water. Guardian spirit and spiritual expression of the water in the river valley.

Valliniyu, the Airy One: connected to air, superior entity of the air spirits of the river valley.

Eknaton, the Fiery One: connected to fire. Guardian of the domestic fire.

Miller: connected to wood, house spirit of the watermill.

Quadrom: house spirit of the upper floor of the watermill, responsible for the heating.

Kollii, the One from the Marsh: marsh spirit, connected to damp woodland, guardian spirit of the marsh wood.

Gnunno, the Green One: connected to plants and trees, superior entity.

The Brown One: connected to the barn animals. Guardian spirit of the barn animals of the region.

Oakbeena: connected to oak trees. Guardian spirit of the oaks in the village.

Madeleine, Lady of the Pines: connected to pine trees. guardian spirit of the pines on a nearby piece of wasteland.

Moonlight, the Silver One: connected to silver, previously the guardian spirit of a silver mine in the Harz region.

The Paper Being: connected to paper, spiritual aspect of all paper which carries information.

Knut, the Sand One: connected to sand, smaller brother of the Stone One.

The Little Glassman: guardian of glass on the earthly and fine substance levels.

Kahine, the Salt Child: connected to salt, facet of the salt deposits of the region.

1. Miller: the House Spirit

Wolfgang Weirauch: I would like to thank you all for being here and for speaking with me.

Verena Staël von Holstein: It's the spirit beings who have to express their thanks. With this conversation one of their essential needs of the present time will be satisfied — speaking!

WW: Hello, Miller.

Miller: Hello.

WW: How old are you and where do you come from, where were you born?

Miller: I'm actually a tree spirit and I was born as an oak tree in the Bavarian Forest in 1267. I grew up there and stood as a tree close together with other trees. I was then felled, came to North Germany over a long and wet journey and was installed as a beam in this mill in 1306.

WW: How is a tree spirit born?

Miller: The tree spirit is born at the moment when the acorn sprouts. At that moment, out of the fundamental substance of the tree spirits a new one is created. Before that, tree spirits are on another spiritual level. We are to be found in the etheric body of the earth, and then we emerge from it.

WW: Does such a tree spirit then remain connected to the felled oak and the beams made out of it?

Miller: Yes, and in fact until the beams have completely decomposed.

WW: What were the people like in the thirteenth century? In what way were they different compared to the people from nowadays?

Miller: Humans were quite different then. They were more like herd animals. They had different eyes, they didn't have so much light in their eyes. They had a different smell, they had a group smell. They were rather like a herd of sheep, led by a bellwether. They were like tree branches. The tree had branches, and when the lowest branch broke off, a new one took its place. But the humans always stayed in the same group form. I experienced the humans of the thirteenth century as groups, as members of a tribe.

WW: And what are they like nowadays?

Miller: Nowadays humans are all like single trees.

WW: And which do you like better, Miller?

Miller: I like the present-day humans better.

WW: Why?

Miller: Because it's right like that.

WW: In what way are you connected to this mill?

Miller: I'm the house.

WW: Can you talk a little about your tasks in this house?

Miller: Yes, gladly. I make sure that the house stays a house. I make sure that it doesn't fall apart, that the floor stays level and that the beams stay straight — the beams are my most important task. That's what I'm here for, to check everything. I check everything in my house everyday, every single bit of it from top to bottom. Looking to see whether a particular piece is still usable, whether the humans still need it or whether I still need it. There's a qualitative difference, you see, between the two of them.

Then I look after the contact with the neighbours. On the one hand that's the humans, on the other hand it's, for example, Echevit, the Watery One. This contact with the neighbouring spheres has to be good. Those are my main tasks, and it's a full programme.

WW: Where does the name Miller come from?

Miller: I thought it up myself.

WW: Why?

Miller: Because it fits.

WW: Do you play practical jokes on humans?

Miller: Of course. It's fun. We trip them up, for example or tip something over. What I like doing is cooking. Cooking is exciting. I`d love to eat something myself just once. But unfortunately, that's not possible.

WW: What happens when you cook? What do you perceive when someone cooks? What do you perceive when someone eats?

Miller: I have experienced how humans cooked in former times. And how they cook nowadays. A few things have changed along the way. How plants and animals become food is quite a special process. You almost always use fire. You then connect love or the spiritual world with the food. As a result the food is radically altered. Observing this process helps me to understand a lot about the processes of change. Besides, it's simply fun to make something beautiful. When the food is good, it helps humans. On the other hand, when it's badly cooked, it makes the body sick.

This interplay between food and health and illness is similar to how a house is constructed. If humans understood better how to consider the body like a house, they wouldn't abuse it so much. That's what they're doing all the time when they feed the body with strange substances. When you drink coffee you make your nerves sore. As a house spirit I can see it. They become red.

WW: So I should drink less coffee?

Miller: It's all the same to me.

WW: What does it mean when the nerves become red?

Miller: That they're not healthy, that they can't function as well as when they're green.

You shouldn't identify your body with the other parts of your being. You humans make lots of mistakes here. The body is important, it provides a house for the human, and the worst thing you can inflict on the body is smoke. when you bring smoke into the body, you bring death into it. Smoke is the worst thing for the body — cigarettes, or whatever you call them. With cigarettes you're attempting to make something physical even more physical. You change your very own personal house with food. That's very exciting for us to watch, especially when this house is made more beautiful.

WW: What's it like for you having the desire for food but not being able to eat?

Miller: It smells so good. And that's why sometimes I'd like to be able to taste it. I can perceive smells, but not flavour. We spirit beings can't eat. We can't perform this kind of transformation of food, but would love to do it sometime.

WW: Would you like to be human just once, for a day?

Miller: Yes and no. To some extent. Although I don't believe I can become a human. But it may happen sometime.

WW: With which spirit beings are you friends?

Miller: With Echevit, the Watery One, with Kapuvu, the Stone One, and for a very long time with the Brown One. Though even longer with Echevit. Echevit was before me and will exist after me. I'm actually friendly with everyone. For some time we've had the Silver Being here, who is beautiful! I didn't know metals could be so beautiful.

WW: Can you leave this house? And when you leave does your being become thinner?

Miller: I can leave the house, but that's not good for the house. I can enter a piece of wood and with the piece of wood be taken anywhere. Every now and again I do this and go somewhere with my humans, and especially when they're doing something exciting.

WW: What happens to the house during your absence?

Miller: I appoint the two deputies directly beneath me and increase their responsibilities for the period of my absence. But my absence can't be for too long. It depends mainly on the stars how long I can be absent.

WW: How long can your absence from the house be?

Miller: At most 62 hours. However for some periods it's just not possible.

WW: Could it happen that you couldn't get back to this house, if, for example, the piece of wood in which you travelled, got burned?

Miller: Yes.

WW: Does the wood have to be carried back by the humans?

Miller: Yes.

WW: So you have to make an agreement with the humans, guaranteeing they'll bring you back to the house again?

Miller: Yes. I can trust my humans.

WW: What do you call the powers of evil?

Miller: The Other Ones.

WW: How do you keep the Other Ones, for example, demons, away from this house?

Miller: By the fact that I'm stronger.

WW: Can you explain to me in greater detail what happens when the Other Ones approach the house?

Miller: The Other Ones mainly try to destroy the works of humans. Why that's so doesn't actually interest me. The Other Ones are responsible for that. Good, aspiring humans live here in this mill, and that's why it's a particular concern of mine to put as many obstacles in the way of the Other Ones as possible.

WW: Why do the Other Ones want to destroy the works of humans?

VS: He's actually shrugging his shoulders

WW: Was this an unusual question?

VS: It seems relatively meaningless to him.

WW: Why?

Miller: The reason it seems meaningless to me, is because these connections have no meaning whatsoever for me and don't concern me. What concerns me is repulsing the Other Ones, as far as I can. When the Other Ones are inferior to me, I can repulse them, but the whys and wherefores of these connections are human questions. It's necessary that I repulse the Other Ones, therefore I do it.

WW: How can a human recognize in a house, whether the Other Ones have gained entry?

Miller: A human can recognize that relatively easily. If you enter a house where you feel uncomfortable, then something isn't right with the structure. And when something isn't right then the Other Ones are always present. Chaos is the characteristic of the descending powers, the Other Ones. The ascending powers bring form, otherwise there could be no ascending development.

WW: Does every house have a house spirit?

Miller: Yes and no. There are houses which are so bad that no house spirit wants to move in there.

WW: I have just been in Afghanistan and saw tens of thousands of destroyed houses in Kabul. Do these houses also have a house spirit?

The High One: In Afghanistan there is a very high number of homeless house spirits, and that is one of the biggest problems for that country. An ancient cultural landscape exists there. But haunted castles are being built there now, haunted astral castles, which lead to the humans living there having to absorb this ghost substance. This haunting however can bring positive changes. Destruction also carries with it the possibility of creating something new. Something new can develop out of the old values. These values are preserved in the respective localities and it's the task of the locality to preserve what's happened there. In the regions of Afghanistan from which the Persian culture migrated northwards, humans have to revive the ancient culture, so that it stands and shines, then something new and great can grow there.

Besides, such questions are too much for the beings here, apart from me.

VS: The High One always chips in when a question comes up, which the others can't answer.

WW: Miller, can you please describe whether you have different tasks for the various days of the week?

Miller: Yes, of course. The days of the week correspond to spiritual principles, and of course, I do something different on a silver day as on Sunday. It's very bad, that humans have forgotten which day the week begins with.

WW: You mean that the week begins with Sunday.

Miller: Yes. The week begins with the light. Sunday is the light. The week is planned out in the quietness of Sunday. I don't do much on this day because I allow the forces from above to work into me. I wait for the light, for ideas.

On Monday I look back and reflect upon the ideas from Sunday which have trickled down from out of the cosmos. Tuesday is the day of action and new concerns are addressed. They're discussed on Wednesday, because the first mistakes have shown up. Hopefully things have become quiet again on

Thursday. On Friday I have to be beautiful, and on Saturday ...

WW: ... review!?

Miller: No. As a matter of fact we do have a review, but primarily we destroy what should be destroyed. Naturally only things which are wrong are destroyed. In other words we have a clear-out.

WW: Every now and then in your book project you all speak about your shelter. What is your shelter, your refuge?

Miller: That's the folded-up side of me, the point at which and in which I can't be touched from the outside. It's the point at which I go through reality on to the other side. I go into the non-ether.

WW: Where is your refuge?

Miller: In the mill.

WW: And where in the mill?

Miller: Everywhere in the mill. When I sleep I stretch myself out for example, somewhere in the mill, or I lie down with my humans in bed. But when I go into the refuge I don't sleep. I turn myself inside out. That's like turning a square inside out so it becomes a cross. I move the outer surface inwards and the inner surface outwards. Then I'm in anti-space and can regenerate myself.

WW: And what do you do when you sleep?

Miller: Then I relax.

WW: How often do you sleep, how often do you wake up?

Miller: At night I'm active in a different way from during the day, and my activity during the night can be compared to the state of sleep in humans. However I don't go all that often into the refuge; mainly Sundays.

WW: And is the amount of sleep on a percentage basis roughly the same as with humans?

Miller: Roughly.

WW: Can you describe space itself, the space in which we humans live?

Miller: Which space do you mean?

WW: The space of physical reality.

Mill weir

Miller: I don't really understand the question.

WW: In the physical-material world, for example, two people can't sit on one chair, whereas spirits interpenetrate. And everything of a physical-material nature is subordinate to the laws of space. I mean this space.

Miller: That's different for us, because two of us can sit without any difficulty on one chair. For me space is what I take care of. Space is that which includes my house, and that also involves the physical space, about which you humans have your ideas. Everything which is enclosed by matter is space. Matter needs space, Matter can't exist without space. You know that.

WW: Of course, but during interviews I often ask questions to which I already know the answers.

Do you have a different feeling when you change from your space into anti-space?

Miller: Yes.

WW: Can you describe it?

Miller: That's difficult with human words. I go through the light. And then I no longer exist. It's like total peace. This description is perhaps the most fitting if humans are meant to understand it. And then I hand over responsibility.

WW: And when you hand over your responsibility, do you hand it over to your two deputies?

Miller: Yes, always these two. And when they have their quiet time, I take over their responsibilities.

WW: And they don't make any mistakes?

Miller: Sometimes, yes.

WW: And what do you do to them, then? Do you tell them off?

Miller: So to speak. It's not that much different with you humans. I then have to straighten things out again.

WW: When you're carrying out a task in the house are you always completely concentrated when doing it, or can you also simultaneously think about something else? Though I don't know if thinking is the right word.

Miller: Yes, thinking is the right word. We do think. We also share in thoughts of a universal nature. I can answer your question with both yes and no, for it depends on the task. If it's something difficult, I'm totally present. I can finish something on the side, only when it's a routine matter.

WW: That's just like humans.

Miller: Yes, we're not very dissimilar to each other.

WW: Can you imagine seeing with human eyes only the physical-material world, but not the spiritual world?

Miller: I've already tried it, and found it boring.

WW: How did you do it?

Miller: I looked through Verena's eyes. A very unsatisfying activity.

WW: Is it probably as though the greater part of your world were to disappear?

Miller: Exactly. But it's got one advantage, because you see the beauty of the material world better. For there's not just an inner beauty, but an outer one as well, This I learned through seeing as a human sees. Perhaps it's comparable to the difference between human seeing and looking. When we see how you see, then we're seeing our deeds for the first time from the outside, other than that, we're looking. Looking includes the spiritual. With your physical eyes you see very little.

WW: What kind of beings are humans for you?

Miller: That's a difficult question. Which humans do you mean? My humans here are very familiar to me. We live together, we're a family, not biologically but spiritually. Most other humans don't interest me. You interest me at the moment, because you're in my house. Then there's another human in Hamburg, who also interests me, because he has to do with this house. I'm envied by other nature-beings, because my humans work with me.

WW: No doubt there are hardly any humans who interact with their house spirit with such awareness.

Miller: There aren't any. A normal human can do much to help a house spirit, even if he doesn't see him. For example, every now and then he can put something nice for him down somewhere. And then he should say, "That's for you. I think it's nice. And that's why I'm putting it here for you."

WW: What do you like the best?

Miller: I like best what the human likes best. That's a very important point. If a human likes to drink water a lot, he should put some water out somewhere for the house spirit. If he's extremely fond of drinking champagne, he should put a glass of champagne out for him. On the other hand, if he likes eating rusks, then he should leave a piece of rusk for the house spirit. It can also be caviar. It doesn't matter what it is, but how it's been given. I share your sympathies and antipathies. When you are friendly towards me, you make me fat and round.

WW: When a human has put some food out for you, what shall he do with it later?

Miller: When it's become mouldy he can throw it away. But if possible, it should stay a while.

WW: How long?

Miller: My humans always leave drinks for as long as it takes them to dry out. I think that's alright. However, if they get covered in horrible layers of mould, they should be thrown away. The minimum is one whole night, the maximum is open.

WW: Is there a house spirit in the house in which I live?

Miller: Yes.

WW: What kind of a house spirit?

Miller: A light-coloured being.

WW: What can I do for him?

Miller: For you it would be best if you would put a cup of coffee out for him, but please, very sweet, for that's what he prefers.

WW: How old is this house spirit?

Miller: Three hundred years.

WW: And where does he come from?

Miller: From a place in the Geest region in North Germany, ending in, *-by*. Paaseby, does that exist?

WW: No idea.

Miller: It's very difficult to get the exact name for this place.

WW: Is he a former tree spirit like you?

Miller: No, he's grown out of the stone. He comes out of the bedrock. It has to be a glacial boulder.

WW: And what kind of house spirit lives in the house of my wife?

Miller: He doesn't like you.

WW: Why not?

Miller: Because you annoyed him. You altered something, something to do with a door. He's small, he's tubby, and actually quite good-natured. But he's got it in for you, because you annoyed him. Have you painted a door or something similar?

WW: No idea. I painted the hall around the door white.

Miller: Something about it upset him.

WW: How can I placate him?

Miller: Put some milk chocolate out for him.

WW: When you look now at all humans, where do their strengths lie, where do their weaknesses lie?

Miller: Their strength is freedom, their weakness is being so unaware. They can't handle their own self or ego. They can't differentiate between their etheric body and their ego. Most humans experience their ego as non-existent; they settle for the etheric body. And that is their ultimate weakness.

WW: And how do you experience human freedom?

Miller: Dangerous. According to our investigations human freedom is the fundamental condition for love. For love is only possible on the basis of true freedom. And that's why freedom is so important, for if love never comes the earth cannot become any more than it already is. It remains physical.

WW: Are humans nowadays freer than, for example, in the thirteenth century?

Miller: No, they're not more free, if anything, more imprisoned. But they're more self-aware. Perhaps that lies in them being slightly more aware of their freedom. But because humans are more aware, they're actually more imprisoned. I wouldn't like to be given freedom.

WW: Not even for one day, just to experience it?

Miller: No.

WW: Are you afraid of it?

Miller: Yes.

WW: Could humans also become elemental beings sometime in the future, and could elemental beings also become human sometime?

Miller: Hopefully at sometime the elemental beings will reach a similar level of importance as humans. That's our big hope. And if humans help us, we can achieve it as well. Humans themselves can become ghosts, and the ghosts are very similar to us.

WW: Can you please give an example of that?

Miller: This happens when for example, humans cling too hard to some material object, for instance, a house. Then they can't get away from this house. Their physical body dies, but the higher parts of their being can't rise into heaven. Then they hang around in a semi-etheric, semi-spiritual state here on the earth. These are ghosts and they're no use to anyone.

WW: Are these the so-called haunted spirits in old houses and castles?

Miller: Yes.

WW: Are there many of them?

Miller: Many more than you think. And they're all very unhappy. For they belong to no one.

WW: But they're no longer humans, just what's left of them.

Miller: Yes, of course, but somewhere in the background a self, an ego still exists.

WW: Can a living person help these haunted spirits?

Miller: Pray. You should include them in your prayers. And because you pray, you should do it. Once a week is enough.

WW: Thank you for the conversation.

Miller: You're welcome, it was a pleasure.

2. Echevit, the Watery One

Wolfgang Weirauch: Hello, Echevit.
The Watery One: Welcome.
WW: What kind of a being are you, and where do you come from?
The Watery One: I'm a Nix, and I've been living here since the last Ice Age, when the ancient river valley was formed. And — because it's so important for you humans — I can well remember the time when Christ was on the earth. I actually originated out of the primal waters. I emerged during the Ice Age at the formation of the River Elbe and its tributaries.

I'm not a spring nymph, I'm a Nix, therefore I'm not so bound to one place as a spring nymph. A spring nymph can't move away from the spring, the Nix on the other hand can move around over larger areas. I always move along over water and if it's very foggy, I can also move over land. I also live here in the mill and devote my attention to the river flowing next to the mill.

I'm also responsible for the breakwaters in the Elbe. That's one of my special tasks. The breakwaters are very curious beings; the old breakwaters are quite reasonable, whereas the new ones are constantly afraid. And then I have to look after them, especially in these days of so much flooding. I check the high-water levels with the river being and hope humans don't dabble around too much with things. Unfortunately they do that very frequently. Generally speaking I take care of the water balance in the Elbe hinterland. From time to time I also go into the North Sea, where we hold meetings and coordinate the water balance. The wet summer in this year was necessary, because the deeper layers of earth were without water.
WW: What relationship exists between you and the undines and how are responsibilities allocated?
The Watery One: I myself am not an undine, but a Nix. A Nix

belongs neither to the undines nor to the nymphs and nixies. Undines are creatures of a more feminine nature, closer to that which flows and gives birth. I myself am a place and have my focus here in the mill, but live just as much in the surroundings I've just described and for this reason have many other beings in me. If it's necessary, I create them.

WW: Are nixies and nymphs undines?

The Watery One: No, neither of them are undines. Nixies live in salt water, nymphs in fresh water, whereas undines are themselves the water. Nixies and nymphs are beings belonging to the water. They take care of the water, they are a spring, but the undines are the water in the spring. Do you understand that? Undines are also in the plants, undines can be quite small. They are the chemists, and they carry life, whereas I organize life. That's the difference between us.

WW: How far have you travelled? What was your furthest journey?

The Watery One: I've seen the whole world.

WW: But you can't go where there's no water.

The Watery One: An aspect of mine can move with the clouds.

WW: So then you can travel over the desert as a cloud?

The Watery One: Yes. But that's no fun at all.

WW: Why not?

The Watery One: Because it's too dry there. There's no life there.

WW: I've heard you drink seaweed punch. What does that mean?

The Watery One: That's a nice drink and it depends on the lunar cycle. The moon needs nineteen years to return again to the same position and the life cycle of seaweed follows this nineteen year lunar cycle.

The qualities of the Zodiac can be subdivided into twelve parts. However, these don't correspond to the calendar. There are displacements. These qualities, these constellations, correspond to the primary qualities of warmth, air, water and earth.

The seaweed punch has a different quality according to the position of the moon, it tastes differently and has slightly different effects. It warms up, it cools down, it creates light, it creates the chemistry of life for we spirit beings.

WW: How do you carry this seaweed punch?

The Watery One: In a glass, of course in a spiritual glass.

WW: Who drinks this seaweed punch?

The Watery One: Undines, nymphs, nixes and even our humans have drunk it once.

WW: Were they aware of it?

The Watery One: Yes.

WW: Did they notice anything?

The Watery One: It had a very invigorating effect on the humans, almost like an injection of vitamin C.

WW: You were formerly a being of a flowing nature, but then became a nix. How did that happen?

The Watery One: That's the ageing process of water.

WW: I don't understand that.

The Watery One: All flowing processes will one day cease and the earth will dry up. Sclerosis is how you refer to it so beautifully in your language. In this respect there'll be more and more nixes and fewer and fewer undines in the future.

WW: What consequences will that have for the earth?

The Watery One: The earth will be able to dissolve. Life itself can't be dissolved, it can only withdraw and go over to another level of being. Life changes from the earth into another state. And water will follow this process, although not as a physical substance but as the elixir of life. That's the water of life.

WW: How is a rainbow formed?

The Watery One: The heavens open and an angel descends, a higher or a lower one.

WW: In your book you speak about the altered properties of light since the time of Christ. Did the rainbow also have a different combination of colours before the birth of Christ compared to now?

The Watery One: Yes.

WW: Can you give a description?

The Watery One: One colour has been added, purple. Before there wasn't any purple as such. Purple has been added through the descending light.

WW: Through the light of the resurrected Christ then?

The Watery One: Yes, and this process lasted three years.

WW: Do the elemental spirits have different states of consciousness?

The Watery One: It's almost exactly as Miller explained. When I rest, my rest is more complete than Miller's. I too have a refuge, can invert myself, changing the levels of being in the process.

WW: Do you also hand over your responsibilities to deputies when you rest?

The Watery One: Yes and no. The structure of the water beings is somewhat different. I have no other nixes under me. During the time when I'm resting the nix function sleeps and the responsibilities are covered from another region. With Miller the responsibilities are assigned within the house, in my case another nix from far away steps in. An undine can't take on any nix function.

WW: What connection do you have to the upper hierarchies, in other words, to angels and archangels?

The Watery One: A good one. The angels are responsible for humans. Specific archangels organize our areas of responsibility. We're actually in constant contact with these archangels. At times it's clearer, other times it's less clear. It's like a constant flow of data. I sense the wishes of the archangels, and comply with them.

WW: Do you have to do exactly as they tell you?

The Watery One: I have no freedom.

WW: Not even a little bit?

The Watery One: I have a little bit at the moment and that's what makes us water spirits so dangerous.

WW: Can you please describe in which areas exactly your little bit of freedom lies?

The Watery One: The reason for my little bit of freedom is that we no longer have to respect human constructions more than our own.

WW: What does that mean? Are you allowed to destroy them?

The Watery One: Yes, we're allowed to destroy them. And we'll destroy far more of them, the more the natural waterways are altered. If you speak with us we don't have to destroy anything.

We've got nothing against canals, we've just got something against the wrong canals. We've also got nothing against sewerage systems, just something against the wrong sewerage systems. Talk to us, and everything'll be alright!

WW: You should be asked where a drainage system should run and how a river can be straightened where it's necessary?

The Watery One: Yes. Humans knew that in former times without having to understand it with their heads. The mill and all its buildings were built by human hand, but so built that they don't disturb us and so built that we've even set up our place of residence here. New buildings are mostly planned sitting at a desk, and the planners don't take a thorough look at the site. Such a thing can't be any good. But that's just a small example.

WW: Are natural catastrophes such as catastrophic floods also caused by nature-beings?

The Watery One: Yes, but not solely.

WW: I've the impression that disasters due to extreme weather conditions are increasing enormously in recent years. Is that true?

The Watery One: Yes. You can even read about it. The Munich Reinsurance Group has drawn up a list from which the significant increase in the vagaries of the weather can be seen. This is due among other things to the small measure of personal freedom we water beings have, for we're accepting the rules of humans less and less now. And the works of humans are changing rapidly, because they've also become much more free.

WW: Does that also mean that, among other things, you kill humans through natural disasters which you have to or want to cause?

The Watery One: Yes.

WW: How is it for you when you kill humans? Do you care? And is it all the same to you who gets killed in the process?

The Watery One: No. This question is difficult to answer. We're never allowed to kill directly. When we kill, we kill indirectly.

WW: What does that mean precisely?

The Watery One: We never directly attack a human, but only a human structure, and if he's stupid enough to place himself on or in this structure, he's actually committing suicide. Then it's all the same to us.

WW: Now, there are humans who are responsible for decisions which aren't agreeable to you. For instance, a river gets straightened or converted to a canal in a way that's bad for it. Certain officials or political decision-makers are responsible. You then cause a natural disaster, destroy these human structures by, for example, bursting a dyke of a straightened river, people then die through the flooding who are in no way responsible for the river being straightened. They're innocent. And my question is whether that's not terrible for you?

The Watery One: Certainly, but humans are free and can get out of this dangerous situation. We don't cause fire disasters, and water disasters mostly happen in ways that humans still have a chance to survive. But when such a man-behind-the-scenes goes on another sailing trip sometime, then it could turn out to be a pretty terrible experience for him. Such things happen.

WW: Could he then get given a shock to his awareness through the external forces of nature?

The Watery One: Yes.

W.W.: Can you describe a little for us humans the etheric world in which you live?

Verena Staël von Holstein: The Watery One is baffled.

W.W.: Normally we don't see your world, hence the question. Please describe it for those humans who don't see it.

The Watery One: If it were to be described using your terms, then you would speak of soft, runny forms, figures reminiscent of hanging cloth of different hues. In the etheric world there are no clear contours. It's like three-dimensional pictures out of spiritual substance, and we move between these pictures. For you, water is mostly something soft. When you consider water from the inside however, it has something totally structured about it. Water looks like a network of rods, nothing but rods. Coloured rods. Structures of sound which are spatial however. You have to imagine yourself as being inside the music.

WW: In other words, spatial, coloured music.

The Watery One: Yes.

WW: Are there things which you spirit beings know but which you're not allowed to tell humans?

The Watery One: Yes.

WW: Now of course I can hardly ask you which ones.

The Watery One: Feel free. It's for example, things about the being of Christ, you're not allowed to know yet. There are things about the higher parts of your being you're not allowed to know yet, but which we know. And there are various things going on in your body which you're not yet able to know. You're simply not yet that advanced and so there's no sense telling you about them. You'd only get confused and your body would function even worse.

WW: Will humans change very much in the coming years?

The Watery One: Yes.

WW: Will many humans acquire supersensory perception?

The Watery One: In the future many humans will acquire supersensory perception, many children today are already seeing supersensibly. And if this way of perceiving doesn't get trained out of them they'll also hold on to it into later life. Time will gradually become thinner and more transparent as a result.

Mankind will divide itself more and more clearly into two groups, the beautiful and the ugly. In the future beauty will become a necessity of immense importance. It'll emerge from being abstract, as you view it at present, and will become a part of life. Life will be beautiful, it will be meaningful, and it'll not just be frippery to dress beautifully, but beauty itself will become a necessity.

WW: Is the point therefore, that everything that is built and created in the physical world be aesthetically formed?

The Watery One: Things will have to be made beautifully, you won't be able to do it any other way at all. This urge for beauty will be a moral force.

WW: Which deeds cause humans to come in the one group or the other?

The Watery One: "Ceaselessly seeking to aspire" *(Faust).* These humans come in the one group. And those not "ceaselessly seeking to aspire," come in the other group. Of course, a certain length of time will be necessary to be able to go from one group into the other.

WW: For how many lives, for how many incarnations, will this change still be possible?

The Watery One: I'm not allowed to answer.

WW: Can one already see today which humans belong or will belong to which group?

The Watery One: Yes. The ones are recognized by their beauty. Beauty means humans really making themselves beautiful, even their outer body. They have to understand in one life on earth the meaning and the necessity of beauty, and then between death and rebirth they'll imprint their new body with an awareness for beauty. And future generations will simply be more beautiful, even outwardly. That's actually quite easy to understand.

WW: Has the length of time between individual human incarnations become shorter? Are humans in our time returning faster to a new life on earth as previously?

The Watery One: The sequence of incarnations is very fast at the moment, so that humans can experience the drastic changes in these times. In addition humans who died young in the many recent appalling wars, get the chance to return rapidly to the earth. For this reason, humans currently incarnating will understand beauty relatively quickly, or will already be bringing it with them into their incarnation. You'll be able to see this beauty physically in them.

WW: Is it a law that those humans who die young also reincarnate quickly?

The Watery One: It's currently so, not at other periods.

WW: What things in the present do the many incarnated humans want to experience?

The Watery One: The return of Christ in the etheric world, the revelation of the ascension into the etheric world. Furthermore they want to experience the coming of the Alien and the appearance in the outer world of Ahriman. The era of Lucifer has gradually come to a close and the principal evil being — in this context the term is important — is at present Ahriman. It's a contemporary distortion that many humans today already consider Lucifer to be a positive being becauses he fires them up with enthusiasm and doesn't leave them cold.

WW: Will Ahriman incarnate in a human body?

The Watery One: Yes and no. No human physical body can carry a being like Ahriman over a longer time. He is so inimical to life that it'll be more like an incorporation.

WW: When will this incarnation or incorporation of Ahriman be?

The Watery One: I'm not allowed to say.

WW: And where will he appear?

The Watery One: In Europe.

WW: Were the humans who are now living, already on the earth a short time ago?

The Watery One: Yes, many. (That's true, for example, of many anthroposophists.) But you always have to consider individual karma.

WW: Can you perceive the chain of incarnations of individual humans?

The Watery One: If I want, yes.

WW: What is time and how does time come into being?

The Watery One: Time comes into being through human consciousness. Human consciousness needs time in order to arrange the things of the world into an order. Time in the generic sense is something completely different, but the terms are lacking in most languages.

WW: Please try to explain more.

The Watery One: Time is a space full of possibilities. You have to imagine time like a space not as a fourth axis or fourth dimension as in mathematics. That's nonsense. Time corresponds more to a construct like your three-dimensional space, it's just that this construct is round. I know, such an idea gives you a headache! But you did ask. There are events in this construct which change the structure of time. And that's history — events within time.

The beings existing in a state of permanence, to whom I don't belong, have a totally different existence. The only two beings in our community who you'll get to know here, who can also live in permanence, are the Fire Spirit and the High One. Both are not just from this world.

WW: Can one as a human create time and destroy time?

The Watery One: Yes. You create time when you complete your work with joy. You'll also create time when you complete unpleasant or menial jobs with pleasure or with joy. If for example, you enjoy scrubbing the floor because it has to be done, then you create time. If you force yourself to do this work and only always thinking that you'll never be finished, time will be destroyed

Sometimes we can give time to humans, if we consider it necessary. And we do it too.

WW: How then?

The Watery One: By inserting a certain period of time.

WW: Does the human notice it?

The Watery One: Some, not all.

WW: Can you explain what love is?

The Watery One: I'm a water being and I know what life is, but not what love is.

WW: What is life?

The Watery One: The necessity of existence on this earth. Life is the possibility of producing permanence. And only through permanence can change be truly brought about.

WW: Thank you for the conversation.

The Watery One: You're welcome, it was a pleasure.

3. Kapuvu, the Stone One

Wolfgang Weirauch: Next I'd like to speak to Kapuvu, the Stone One. Are you there?

The Stone One: I'm always there.

WW: Hello.

The Stone One: Hello.

WW: What kind of a being are you, and what tasks do you have?

The Stone One: I've been a stone and I'll also have been a stone, depending on where you'll have had looked. If you shall have had problems with my use of verbs I'll make the effort to have spoken more slowly.

WW: Why do you speak in this curious mixture of tenses? It reminds me of an echo effect.

The Stone One: Because it's necessary if you exist as matter. Matter has always been been, otherwise it couldn't be.

WW: So you want to express with your language a connection between past, present and future?

The Stone One: Yes. I'll also have used the pure present form. That's always had a special significance. It's then always in accordance with the spirit of matter. But this form is also sometimes necessary so that you'll understand me correctly.

WW: What relationship do you have to the gnomes?

The Stone One: They are the smallest aspects of my being. Where I am, they must have always been been. Gnomes are beings of necessity, like goblins.

WW: How does a stone being come into being? Or can a stone being come into being at all, since it's always been there?

The Stone One: I've always been there.

WW: You've never come into being?

The Stone One: Never is a term which in regard to actual matter will have had no meaning. Has death always been there, or will it always be there, or one day will there have been death no more?

WW: The time will come when death will exist no more.

The Stone One: Then matter has also been necessary no more. Then matter will never have been in existence.

WW: How is a stone being connected to a physical stone?

The Stone One: I am the stone!

WW: Can you ...?

The Stone One: No.

WW: I haven't even asked my question yet.

The Stone One: You wanted to have asked whether I can ever leave a stone. — No, I can't. I'm *always* there and always connected to a stone.

WW: Can you travel?

The Stone One: No.

WW: Not even when someone takes a stone with him?

The Stone One: No.

WW: In what place do you live?

The Stone One: I'm connected to the whole earth, to the matter of the whole earth, I can have reduced myself to the size of an atom, in order to have been at a certain place for you. Normally I've been as large as the surface of this place has been.

WW: But you can spread yourself over the whole earth?

The Stone One: Yes.

WW: You can now be both in Africa as well as here?

The Stone One: Yes.

WW: What happens to a stone being when a stone is worked by a human?

The Stone One: I then change myself.

WW: Can you describe in detail what changes with you?

The Stone One: In many respects I can have described that. If a person like Michelangelo has worked on a block of marble, the stone has become beautiful. The being of the stone has then also become beautiful. In exactly the same way we could have been made ugly.

WW: How?

The Stone One: Through humans working on a stone. Stones suffer when they're crushed to sand. That's the most unpleasant thing that can have been done to us. We've been stone, compact, not sand.

WW: What happens when a stone is split or shattered?

The Stone One: It depends. If it's fallen down from a rock face, through weathering, rain, snow or wind, a part of the stone beings go into the earth, a part of the beings who have been in this stone, will have been earth. The remainder is then a smaller stone being.

WW: Are you also connected to artificial stones which humans manufacture for building their houses?

The Stone One: Yes, unfortunately. Distorted stone beings arise as a result.

WW: How are earthquakes generated?

The Stone One: Through the movement of the larger stone beings.

WW: And when are earthquakes generated?

The Stone One: When it's necessary.

WW: And when is it necessary?

The Stone One: When the forces in the interior of the earth have to have been differently distributed, when something in the love of the earth had changed.

WW: Are humans responsible when an earthquake occurs?

The Stone One: Sometimes.

WW: Can you explain that a bit more in detail? Through which human failings can an earthquake be caused?

The Stone One: Sometimes an earthquake will have occurred so that other humans in this region will be helped. The earth beings have caused an earthquake so that aid can be brought in, that awareness for a devastated region will be emerged.

WW: So that the poor humans of this region, therefore, who have survived the earthquake, will be helped.

The Stone One: So has it been.

WW: Earthquakes often affect humans in poorer regions.

The Stone One: That's why!

WW: But many innocent humans also die in the process.

The Stone One: Perhaps they would have had died from hunger anyway. Death *is* nothing other than Matter itself has been.

WW: Will there be further and stronger earthquakes in the next few years on the earth?

The Stone One: It will have been not necessarily stronger ones, but it will have been many.

WW: Will there be further changes in the earth?

The Stone One: For what period of time have you now asked?

WW: For the next twenty to thirty years.

The Stone One: Very few.

WW: Do you stone spirits have any sympathy for those humans who have been injured or killed in an earthquake? Or couldn't you care less?

The Stone One: What is sympathy?

WW: Humans experience pain, they suffer, and my question is whether you can share this pain. Through earthquakes individual humans lose their husband, or their wife or their children, and that's painful for them.

The Stone One: Humans take stones and make sand out of them. Have humans experienced sympathy for us, as they've done that?

WW: No, they haven't.

The Stone One: And because of that we should have had sympathy with them?

WW: I don't know, it was just my question.

The Stone One: I've answered. We stone beings *are* dead. Does death have sympathy?

WW: You are dead?

The Stone One: We are dead, because we have been and will have been Matter. Death corresponds spiritually to matter. From your point of view death is very living.

WW: Can you say something about what happens at those places in the earth where rocks combine with metal ores? Is something special taking place there?

The Stone One: Yes! There's been quite a lot going on there! Metal beings from outside enter into the earth. This process has still not yet been completed. Metal beings stream through the earth in rhythmic paths. You've called these veins. These paths will have been especially embraced by us. Metal beings have been the correspondence to the planets, which the earth will have been and has been.

WW: What relationship do you have to the metal beings?

The Stone One: A good one.

WW: In your book project you speak about two groups of humans who will gradually emerge, the good and the evil. When did you notice for the first time that two such groups are emerging?

The Stone One: The dead have been different.

WW: To what extent?

The Stone One: They have been brighter. The dead have been brighter from the ones of beauty.

WW: They were more full of light?

The Stone One: Yes, and this light is brighter.

WW: Every human has a guardian angel. When mankind divides itself into a good and an evil group, do the guardian angels of these humans also divide themselves into two groups?

The Stone One: I can't have answered that. Please ask the High One that.

WW: Thank you.

The Stone One: You're welcome. Have had a good journey. With Christ!

WW: Is it difficult to speak with the Stone One?

Verena Staël von Holstein: He's quite exhausting, but I've got quite a special relationship to him since I've put down roots here myself in the watermill. He's both old and young. When you consider fire, stone is quite young. But you can reverse this relationship too by realizing that stone is very old and fire is very young. The Stone One has an incredibly clear and definite point of view.

WW: He seems to be very consistent.

VS: He's incredibly merciless. We've often no awareness of the earth. Most people nowadays understand something about water pollution and air pollution, and they try and do something about it. But most people aren't interested in all the filth which ends up going into the earth and polluting it. We should sometime speak about fire pollution as well.

WW: Stone One, I do still have a few questions. How do you feel about all the poisons from humans ending up in the soil?

The Stone One: I will have felt terrible about it. If humans had thought about everything they've had done to the soil, they'd understand that we ourselves are having to have been transformed with the soil into the spirit matter of Jupiter. A naturally evolved soil helps, a heap of atomic waste and other poisons disturbs the spiritualization process the earth has to have had.

WW: Can the poisoned area of the earth not be spiritually transformed later, does it remain behind as slag?

The Stone One: It can be spiritualized but it will have had demanded quite a lot of strength from humans. Strength which has been much more necessary for other things, such as to have been able to build a bridge over the abyss for other humans. Decisions will have to be made, which are final, and death-like.

WW: In other words humans have to spiritualize the whole earth?

The Stone One: A spiritual image of the earth has to be created, but all of Matter must not be transformed. Waste products will have to remain.

WW: This slag will then orbit Jupiter like a physical moon?

The Stone One: No. I'm not allowed to say.

WW: I was in Chernobyl and saw and visited the contaminated landscape and reactor. What effect does such radioactivity on the earth?

The Stone One: You humans think radioactivity destroys Matter. That isn't quite correct. Then from another angle it creates new matter which is much heavier than the old matter has been been. And this new matter will be considerably harder to have had been spiritually transformed. Natural radioactivity is necessary for certain things, artificial radioactivity produces slag.

Plutonium is especially dangerous. Plutonium is like a dagger, which acts like a hammer.

WW: And it destroys!

The Stone One: Yes, it destroys in order to be made more indestructible. Indissoluble has been the right human word.

WW: In the future will new forms of energy be won from the earth?

The Stone One: Yes, from the earth itself.

WW: What will these forces look like? Can they already be described?

The Stone One: Like the sound of E flat.

WW: Thank you.

The Stone One: You're welcome. With Christ!

4. Valliniyu, the Airy One

Wolfgang Weirauch: Now I'd like to speak with Valliniyu, the Airy One. You say you can't see him. Why not?

Verena Staël von Holstein: He claims it's because I'm too similar to him. That's why I can't see him. I was born in an air sign, Libra. And I'm very connected to the air. In any case I can speak with the Airy One, more than speak with him, but I can't perceive him directly.

WW: Hello. What kind of a being are you, and what tasks do you have?

The Airy One: I'm a wind. My main task is to bring light to the earth, to give light the possibility of reaching the earth. Another task of mine is similar, and that is to carry the world, to carry for example, pollen and clouds. And clouds are beings, but you know that.

WW: How old are you, and when were you born?

The Airy One: There are no terms in your language for that.

WW: So old?

The Airy One: Yes, older than you think.

WW: Can you say something about how storms arise?

The Airy One: At the moment many storms are being produced in order to transport thoughts from Central Europe into the Middle East. One of the tasks of storms is to carry thoughts. On the other hand storms are being produced at the present to stimulate the water. This happens in agreement with the higher water spirits and us. Certain information comes from the warmth sphere, which we air spirits receive, and we transmit this information via the air currents to the water. Finally it's the turn of the stone beings, who receive this information, and form the structures of the earth out of it. Here the activity of the hierarchies, who initiate this process, meets the activity of the elemental spirits. This occurs because the intentions of the individual beings meet.

WW: Can you explain a bit more in detail which thoughts are transported from Central Europe to the Middle East?

The Airy One: All of them. The good as well as the evil, the complicated as well as the simple.

WW: And why are the thoughts transported from Central Europe over to the Middle East?

The Airy One: They're the ones which will be the next bearers of human culture. At present it's the turn of the humans in Central Europe. They're now getting old, and the young humans from Eastern Europe and the Middle East are moving here.

WW: Why don't the thoughts move the other way?

The Airy One: It's humans who move the other way. Humans always move towards the thoughts. Humans as a mass always migrate towards the thoughts. Thoughts go from the old to the new, and humans move from the new to the old. That has to be so. That's a fundamental law of development for the earth.

WW: Since when have these thoughts been moving from Europe to the Middle East.

The Airy One: For a few years. The drastic change was a short while age. There was a struggle in the hierarchies which made it possible.

WW: How did the winds move before?

The Airy One: They moved around the whole world and prepared for globalization. Globalization is a process which seen from the spiritual plane is already completed.

WW: How are you connected to the sylphs?

The Airy One: Sylphs are the small, delicate beings, who care for the plants at a local level and foster the flowers. Sylphs are like sisters of mine.

WW: How are air and light connected?

The Airy One: They're principally the same. The one is an aspect of the other. If you look from the one side, it's air, if you look from the other side, it's light.

WW: How dependent is the activity of the sylphs on the conditions of the air and the light?

The Airy One: The dependence is great. Sylphs are the messengers of the light on a small scale. Sylphs aren't large beings. Speaking in human terms they're smaller than humming birds. They're also dependent on the positions of the stars. For example, Uranus as a planet of light has wandered in front of a light constellation, Aquarius. That's been happening for a few months, and since then the sylphs are active in other ways. Many humans have noticed what's happening with Uranus by the fact that they get a headache by sitting in the sun although the sun wasn't shining strongly. These are the effects of Uranus. These effects are very strong and in certain spheres cause a kind of over-reaction. You'll notice it when you look at the flowers. In this year they're partly out of shape, sometimes in very funny forms.

WW: Can you say something about how the light has changed through the resurrection of Christ?

The Airy One: It's become more colourful.

WW: Has the physical air also changed since then?

The Airy One: Of course.

WW: How?

The Airy One: Its composition has altered, in fact so much that shortly before the birth of Christ, people with present-day lungs would not have been able to live without suffering harmful effects. They would have suffered asthma attacks.

WW: How is the air altered through air pollution and what does it mean for the nature spirits?

The Airy One: For the spirit beings it means much more work because the plants must nevertheless grow and in the zone close to the plants we have an enormous increase in work load. Plants themselves are innocent. And one of our most important tasks is to ensure the plants suffer as little as possible from air pollution. That means that in a very thin zone as thin as a sylph, the air around the plants is still good. That's why it's so much more pleasant to breathe in a wood. We do what we have to, and give the filth in the air on to the water. And, just imagine, you don't just pollute the air, but also the light.

WW: With what?

The Airy One: With air pollution. That's at the same time a pollution of the light. Wisdom corresponds spiritually to light. And when the air is polluted through human deeds — this happens through deeds of the earth as well, for example, through volcanic eruptions with dust and such like, then what the air brings, the wisdom of heaven in the light, reaches the earth in a polluted form.

WW: Is light polluted also by thoughts?

The Airy One: Yes, of course. That can be done.

WW: Can you say something about what the aurora is?

The Airy One: The aurora is a part of the visible language of the angels.

WW: Do the angels want to communicate something to humans with the aurora?

The Airy One: Yes and no. They want to show beauty to one another, and they want the spiritual world not to be forgotten. People who live under the northern lights are more likely to have the ability to perceive nature-beings. People in Iceland for example, still see the "wee folk." That's also connected to the aurora.

WW: What's taking place at present in the etheric sphere of the earth?

The Airy One: A lot. Everything that's connected to the birth of the Christ in the etheric. And that's what we're working on now. This birth has already taken place, but till now has remained relatively unnoticed. Only very few humans have noticed it. Through this birth new light, in fact etheric light, has come to the earth. This light has to be woven into the being of the world.

WW: What can humans do so that this etheric light gets woven in.

The Airy One: Use cars less.

WW: What else?

The Airy One: Pray. Praying nearly always helps.

WW: How do the air beings or the sylphs receive the planetary forces, and how do they pass them on to humans and plants?

The Airy One: We receive the planetary forces out of the warmth which encompasses the earth and which is actually the sun. The sun is a being of warmth and in a spiritual sense is the Christ, at least a part, a cosmic aspect of His being. The wisdom is taken from this sphere and this wisdom is transmitted to the earth.

WW: Is there also celestial music?

The Airy One: Yes.

WW: Can you please describe it a bit?

The Airy One: You hear it every night. But you humans can't remember. But the time will come. Listen to Mozart, he comes closest to this celestial music.

WW: How does the celestial music arise and what effect does it have on you?

The Airy One: We air beings aren't so interested in the music. We transport it to the earth. The musical tones draw the angels closer and that's also beautiful. Water is more like music. Glass is coagulated music.

WW: Is there a difference between the music humans create with acoustic instruments and the electronic music coming out of the loudspeaker?

The Airy One: There's an enormous difference. It depends on the place. Music is only real when it sounds at the place where it's played. Music has a character specific to place. When music is reproduced on a CD it isn't harmful, but it really isn't music anymore, more like sound. Music is only music at the moment of its creation. But electronically produced music is harmless.

WW: It'll certainly amaze many that you nature spirits are familiar with electronically produced music.

The Airy One: We have to carry it. You're constantly saddling us with it.

WW: Do you know any films, such as *Star Wars?*

The Airy One: Yes.

WW: What do you think about it?

The Airy One: George Lucas brought many thoughts, good thoughts into a form so that they have been transmitted effortlessly to many people. Film is moreover an appropriate contemporary medium for bringing good thoughts to people. That applies especially to *Star Wars.* It doesn't apply to all science fiction films in general.

WW: Are there people who spread a kind of astral stench?

The Airy One: Yes.

WW: Can you describe this a little?

The Airy One: Reluctantly.

WW: Why reluctantly?

The Airy One: Because it stinks. If I describe this stench, I have to sort of produce it. When a human has a destructive disposition, the same thing happens on the spiritual plane as in a corpse on the physical plane. And it stinks just as much for us too.

WW: What effect do the evil thoughts of humans have in the spiritual world?

The Airy One: They produce evil beings. Every thought corresponds to a being. We have contact with all beings which are produced. And when evil beings are produced we have stress — expressing it in human terms. Every thought is a being.

WW: What happens when a person meditates or prays?

The Airy One: When he meditates he spiritually forms a tree. When he prays he speaks with the spiritual world. What else should happen? It's like a channel to heaven.

WW: I thought that more light gets radiated through meditation or prayer.

The Airy One: In the channel is light, and the tree also produces light, yes. That's obvious.

WW: Is every thought which has been thought by a person, recorded in the world ether?

The Airy One: Every one of them.

WW: And does it always remain there?

The Airy One: Always. For as long as I'm alive, it's been so.

WW: If a person wrongly thinks a thought, does this thought then have to be correctly thought in order to balance out the wrong thought?

The Airy One: It doesn't work like that. Thoughts can be erased, but the erased spot will be seen nevertheless.

WW: Thoughts, which are thought by people, are these imprints in the etheric world or are they also beings?

The Airy One: Both.

WW: In other words, every thought someone thinks becomes a being?

The Airy One: Yes, and is at the same time an imprint.

WW: A person can't think at all without creating elemental beings?

The Airy One: That's the way it is, and these beings are all related to the air beings. That's why it's especially important for us that people finally come to understand this. That goes for every simple thought. When someone thinks about getting a ticket out of a ticket machine, then they create a ticket being. And that also goes for every absurd and false thought.

WW: It would therefore be reasonable for people to take more responsibility for their own thoughts?

The Airy One: That would be very reasonable.

WW: Then it must be really teeming with these beings, there must be an infinite amount of them.

The Airy One: Yes.

WW: Isn't it terrible for you that so many absurd and evil thought beings are being produced?

The Airy One: Very.

WW: Do you do away with these beings, do you sort them or what do you do with them?

The Airy One: We shake them up, we try to sort them and they're partly not even capable of living. Many of them are quite small but then they aren't that disturbing.

WW: Will these beings exist for ever?

The Airy One: They fade. If it's a ticket being, then it fades and does so in a relatively short time, and becomes a general thought mush, if I may be allowed to put like that it in your peculiar language.

WW: But important thoughts remain in existence longer?

The Airy One: Much longer. There are thoughts which are very old.

WW: Which is the oldest thought?

The Airy One: "In the beginning was the Word."

WW: How far does your sphere of activity reach?

The Airy One: As far as the limits of the Sun being. Beyond Pluto there is another planet. We've also given it a name, which however isn't very nice, and that's Erebos. Our sphere of activity reaches as far as that.

WW: What kind of a planet is Erebos?

The Airy One: Erebos is very cold. It corresponds outwardly to the earth. It's the first place where the alien will land.

WW: Is the alien Ahriman?

The Airy One: No.

WW: Who then?

The Airy One: I can't say the name.

WW: Do you mean Sorath?

The Airy One: No.

WW: What task does the alien have?

The Airy One: Ask the High One.

WW: Thank you for the conversation.

The Airy One: You're welcome.

WW: The Airy One is very fast.

VS: He's so fast that sometimes I can hardly get across everything he says.

WW: He made a completely different impression from the Stone One. As you transmitted the thoughts of the Stone One you spoke very slowly, with the Airy One it went chop, chop.

I noticed you were already receiving an answer from the spirit being while I was still putting my question. At the moment when I'm formulating my question, do you already have the answer? At what moment when I'm putting my question do the spirit beings know what I'm asking? Here I'm thinking especially of questions which I'm not fully aware of, and for which I have to take another look at what's on my sheet of paper.

VS: They already know everything while you're asking, in fact with the first word of your question. And that's also when I receive the answer.

5. Eknaton, the Fiery One

Wolfgang Weirauch: Then on to the Fiery One. Hello, Eknaton.
The Fiery One: Hello.
WW: Can you say something about your being?
The Fiery One: I am the flame.
WW: What tasks do you have?
The Fiery One: I burn. That's my main task. In contemplating me humans are able to look directly into the spiritual world. When you look into a flame you look into the spiritual world. Directly. Furthermore I heat various things. In addition I'm the symbol of love, for warmth is love. Moreover I cause the fruit to ripen, and that's an enormous and complex task. In the different seasons of the year, in so far as it's in accordance with the positions of the planets, I weave warmth around the world. The fruit will then be good. This year there was little warmth and the water beings wove coldness around the world. That's why in this year there won't be a good harvest.
WW: When were you born and how?
The Fiery One: I'm constantly being born. I'm always new. I'm recreated through every flame.
WW: Does your being have no beginning?
The Fiery One: Not in this world.
WW: What relationship do you have to the salamanders?
The Fiery One: They're my brothers.
WW: Are you also a salamander?
The Fiery One: Yes and no.
WW: Why no?
The Fiery One: Because I'm more than a salamander.
WW: Can salamanders and fire beings only live in fire or in other places as well?
The Fiery One: Not just in fire but at least in warmth.
WW: They can never leave the spheres of warmth and fire?

The Fiery One: No, for then they'll no longer exist.

WW: Are they then dead?

The Fiery One: We can't die. We're constantly being born, and that excludes death. It's an endless birth. If you want to kill us, you'd have to kill Christ. But you humans shouldn't try that.

WW: As a fire being what relationship do you have to the other nature-beings?

The Fiery One: They're afraid of me, because I carry the spiritual world directly in me. They're all afraid of me, even the animals.

WW: How do you communicate with the other nature-beings if they're all afraid of you?

The Fiery One: I communicate little with them, and that's my problem. That's why it's nice that I'm getting into conversation here with the other nature-beings. That's something quite rare, because they're normally afraid of me.

WW: Do you keep yourself at the moment somewhat away from the other beings?

The Fiery One: Somewhat. They're there where they always are, but they aren't within my flame.

WW: What would Miller say if you were to burn down this mill? Can something like that happen?

The Fiery One: Yes. But I wouldn't do it for the house-martins are still nesting here.

WW: Can you describe the being of flame and fire a little?

The Fiery One: I can say very much and very little to that. Because a flame is something spiritual nothing material can endure it. Matter and flame are mutually exclusive. Matter can't remain where I am, it can only vanish in the flame. There shines through me what you see every night when you're asleep. Children still know it.

WW: You're not just flame but also warmth. Warmth is in all living bodies. And other beings aren't afraid of warmth.

The Fiery One: That's correct. They're only afraid of me in my pure form. Warmth is another aspect of mine. It can spread itself out, it's also not a material substance. Warmth can also be felt in the soul. In the process of warmth something is indeed transformed, but not matter. As warmth I can be everywhere, for warmth is very, very small. That's why warmth can also get in everywhere, it can permeate everything.

WW: Can you say how lightning originates?

The Fiery One: Lightning originates where the will of the hierarchies actively expresses itself.

WW: What tasks do the fire beings have when lightning flashes?

The Fiery One: They have to accompany the flash and they're swept along by it. Because lightning is the spiritual world in the physical world the fire beings also have to be involved. It won't work any other way.

WW: Is every flash of lightning a being?

The Fiery One: Yes and no. It's a primary being accompanied by many smaller ones. It's one will of many beings.

WW: And when a lightning flash is produced are these beings born and do they disappear again when the lightning ceases?

The Fiery One: We're just born, we don't die. We're then somewhere else again. Then we're warmth.

WW: Why are there more and more thunderstorms recently, especially in this year?

The Fiery One: Because the time has come!

WW: Please explain that more exactly. Why is it the time for thunderstorms?

The Fiery One: Amongst other things it's time because the stars are standing in particular constellations, because human beings are behaving very badly, and because the middle and upper hierarchies are sending their intentions down to the earth in the form of strong impulses.

WW: Through which bad thoughts, feelings and deeds of people is a thunderstorm caused, how are they connected to one another?

The Fiery One: A thunderstorm is caused for example, when groups of people try to exploit other groups of people, exploiting them on an economic level. Unfair trade generates a lot of thunderstorms.

WW: There's quite a lot of unfair trade going on in the course of globalization.

The Fiery One: Exactly.

WW: Do you mean the exploitation of people in the poor countries?

The Fiery One: Yes, exactly. I see you understand me.

WW: Which impulses come through a thunderstorm on to the earth from the will of the hierarchies?

The Fiery One: Ask the High One.

WW: What is eternity, what is time?

The Fiery One: Eternity is the permanence of fire, for you humans and for me. Time is another kind of space. Time comes into existence at the place where the material world is penetrated by the spiritual world in order to cause the material world to come into being or to die away or to change. That's the reason for the existence of time.

WW: Does eternity only exist outside of time or in time as well?

The Fiery One: Every single thing has its own eternity. So long as it exists it is for itself eternal.

WW: Why does a finger get burned when it's held in a flame?

The Fiery One: Because then it touches the spiritual world.

WW: Can you explain that in more detail?

The Fiery One: Matter and the spiritual world can't exist at the same time in one place, at least not yet this form of matter.

WW: What happens to the human etheric body in the case of burns?

The Fiery One: With every burn scars are formed in the etheric body. Every injury to the physical body produces definite scars in the etheric body. In the case of scars originating from burns the etheric body is thinner, in the case of scars originating from other external injuries the etheric body is thicker.

WW: What does that mean? Is the human more sensitive for spiritual things at the places where he has scars from burns or is he weakened there?

The Fiery One: He's more sensitive.

WW: What relationship do the fire beings have to human language?

The Fiery One: Actually none at all.

WW: What relationship do the fire beings have to electricity?

The Fiery One: When we sacrifice ourselves electricity is generated.

WW: How do you sacrifice yourselves for electricity?

The Fiery One: We metamorphose ourselves; it's hard to describe. To a certain extent we die into a deeper material plane.

WW: In other words you become heavy light?

The Fiery One: We become heavy fire.

WW: What's your opinion of the internet?

The Fiery One: It's in accord with the contemporary spirit.

The Stone One: It will have been necessary. The internet is one of the possibilities for the Ahrimanic beings to be able to exist. And these beings are necessary.

WW: What are they necessary for?

The Stone One: To make humans into gods.

WW: But humans have to protect themselves from these beings.

The Fiery One: Yes, of course. They have to overcome them or at least assert themselves in the face of them. They have to remain human. The Ahrimanic beings have no interest in humans remaining human, but are interested in humans falling as far back again as possible to the level of the animals.

WW: When fire beings sacrifice themselves, die into electricity, are they forced to do so by higher beings?

The Fiery One: We're only half-free but we don't suffer any compulsion in the human sense.

WW: Can you say something about how people will slowly become clairvoyant again?

The Fiery One: That'll happen quickly, but most people are afraid of it and for this reason don't understand it.

WW: How is it that more and more people are becoming clairvoyant?

The Fiery One: Because it's necessary.

WW: Necessary for what?

The Fiery One: For the progress of humankind.

WW: What's changing in the human constitution so that they become clairvoyant?

The Fiery One: They're shaking inwardly.

WW: Will people in the near future also acquire other abilities, new abilities of the soul?

The Fiery One: "Obscurvoyance" also exists, in other words the ability to perform great deeds through black magic. That happens when stupid things are done with the chemical forces of the human.

WW: Will more and more people in future be able to perceive who they were in their last life on earth?

The Fiery One: Yes, many children can already do it.

WW: And will humans when they perform some deed already have a kind of preview of the karmic compensation for this deed in some future life?

The Fiery One: If they practise they'll acquire this ability.

WW: Do nature-beings have a memory?

The Fiery One: What for?

WW: You don't need a memory because you always know everything anyway?

The Fiery One: We're spirit beings. We fire beings are very similar to humans. We have an ego-like body. We don't need a memory in the human sense, because we're only ego-like. We have access similar to a memory to the world ether.

WW: Do you always see everything?

The Fiery One: Yes, everything.

WW: Is it pleasant or unpleasant not being able to forget anything?

The Fiery One: We don't know anything else.

WW: But you know people can forget things?

The Fiery One: Yes.

WW: Can you imagine what that's like?

The Fiery One: I ask myself what it's good for.

WW: When someone for example, has experienced something unpleasant and perpetually clings to it, it can disable them very much. When he forgets it, on the other hand, it can also be healing.

The Fiery One: That has no doubt something to do with freedom.

WW: Would you like to be human just once for a short time?

The Fiery One: No.

WW: Why not?

The Fiery One: Because I'm a salamander. I couldn't burn anymore then.

WW: Where do you have your refuge?

The Fiery One: Here in the tiled stove.

WW: And how often do you retire there?

The Fiery One: In summer quite often, because the stove is then out. And there I go into my folded-up state.

WW: And when someone at that moment lights a candle, do you have to come out of your refuge?

The Fiery One: No, a deputy then takes my place.

WW: It can therefore never be that all nature-beings simultaneously seek out their refuges?

The Fiery One: The world would then collapse That's not on.

Verena Staël von Holstein: He found this question quite bizarre.

WW: What relationship exists between fire spirits and love?

The Fiery One: We're an aspect of love, and in fact an aspect of the universal substance of love. We're what remains of love when humans don't manage to create true love. When humans don't manage it, there exists "only" normal fire.

WW: Humans can therefore transform fire into love?

The Fiery One: Yes.

WW: In the process do they also transform a salamander?

The Fiery One: Yes.

WW: Does this salamander become a more advanced being in the process?

The Fiery One: Yes.

WW: And you like it when humans accomplish this transformation?

The Fiery One: Yes, because we ourselves are then love.

WW: You go from a fire being to a being of love?

The Fiery One: Exactly.

WW: What are ice giants?

The Fiery One: They dwell in Niflheim. They're the opposite from us, the dark aspect of fire. Where there's no fire, there's cold. Where it's lukewarm, both are equally represented. Ice giants are large and cold.

WW: Do ice giants have anything to do with human hatred?

The Fiery One: Yes.

WW: Do they come into being through human hatred?

The Fiery One: As well. They're mutually dependent. They existed before humans, but have then become what corresponds to hatred in humans.

WW: Don't the ice giants also have a feeling for nature?

The Fiery One: Just like all of us! We also don't hate one another. One end of a balance doesn't hate the other end.

WW: Can it come about that you fight one another?

The Fiery One: That can happen but it's more of a game. The worst thing that can happen, is everything becoming lukewarm.

WW: Would everything then be unimportant?

The Fiery One: Yes, exactly, everything would then be truly unimportant.

WW: Thank you very much.

The Fiery One: You're welcome. Have a good fire!

6. The Four Groups of Elemental Beings Through the Year

Wolfgang Weirauch: I'd now like to question you four elemental beings about certain things to do with the course of the year and about the plant and animal kingdoms. First of all you again, Eknaton. Can you describe what kind of being spiritually the butterfly is?

The Fiery One: Why don't you ask the Airy One?

WW: Can't you answer this question?

The Fiery One: A butterfly isn't very important to me. The butterfly is a flower which has freed itself from the ground. And the Airy One is responsible for flowers.

WW: Don't fire spirits have a special relationship to insects?

The Fiery One: Yes, if we were to step out into the visible world then we'd be for example, butterflies.

WW: That's exactly what I wanted to hear. But that's quite an intensive relationship, isn't it?

The Fiery One: On the one hand it is, but we're not butterflies so long as we're fire spirits. I'll try and explain. At that moment at which we're forced through the layer, we have to become butterflies. But we're then no longer fire spirits. The air is then responsible for us. And that would also mean we haven't become beings of love. That's why we're afraid of butterflies.

WW: Do butterflies send out a spiritual substance into the cosmos?

The Fiery One: Something similar to light.

WW: Valliniyu, what's the spiritual significance of birds?

The Airy One: The birds are the end of a line of evolution. Their development hasn't continued, they actually shouldn't have become what they are at present. Someone has manipulated their development.

WW: What's the spiritual significance of bats?

The Airy One: Bats have something to do with fire. They do move through the air but they actually fly through a completely different medium. Seen with spirit eyes they look like firework rockets. That's why I always call them fire-bats.

WW: Are bats afraid?

The Airy One: Yes, of humans.

WW: Is there a substance the birds give to the spiritual world when they die?

The Airy One: Yes, that has something of a chemical nature. It looks like thick creamy water. And it shines.

WW: Is there also a substance a flock of bats leaves behind?

The Airy One: Spiritually or physically?

WW: Physically.

The Airy One: They leave ashes behind.

WW: And spiritually?

The Airy One: Embers.

WW: When a person breathes in these embers or ashes, is something altered in him?

The Airy One: He acquires more structure, dark structure. It's like a spider's web being drawn into the human.

WW: Is this spider's web connected to Ahriman?

The Airy One: Yes and no. Both evil powers are involved in this spider's web. The spider's web is the track left by Luciferic and Ahrimanic beings. This substance was formerly more Luciferic, at present it's more Ahrimanic. Bats transport currents coming from out of the dark worlds.

WW: Kapuvu, what activity do you perform together with the gnomes between the mineral forces of the earth and the roots of the plants?

The Stone One: Gnomes are the little ones in my family. They care for the cosmic forces. In autumn they raise the cosmic forces from out of the plant roots, and in the spring they give them back again so that the plants can grow. The important thing for us in this process is the gathering up of the cosmic forces. The other part of the process is a kind of labour of love, inasmuch as we're able to love at all.

WW: The plants gather the cosmic forces into themselves in spring and in summer, and you then preserve them in the earth in autumn and in winter?

The Stone One: That's how it's been, and that's how it will have been.

WW: How do you preserve these cosmic forces in the earth?

The Stone One: We preserve them in the structures of the crystals. There's something like a matrix in crystals and the cosmic forces seep into this matrix. It looks very beautiful.

WW: The earth therefore shines in the winter?

The Stone One: So could it have had been said.

WW: Can you describe in a bit more detail these cosmic forces you preserve in autumn and winter?

The Stone One: They're the thoughts of the archangels.

WW: And do these forces when you push them upwards in the spring, help a new plant to grow?

The Stone One: That has been almost right. We don't push them, the undines do that, and we inform them.

WW: Do gnomes actually love the earth?

The Stone One: Only human beings are having been able to love.

WW: What relationship do gnomes have to toads?

The Stone One: We've been afraid of toads. Toads are how we would have to have had appeared if you could have been able to have seen us with your normal eyes. Toads are quite hideous animals.

WW: Can a gnome become a toad?

The Stone One: Yes and no.

WW: And when yes?

The Stone One: When you look at a toad it's always got something gnome-like about it.

WW: My question was, when can a gnome transform itself into a toad?

The Stone One: When it wants to have been visible. When it wants to have had felt life in the human, in the physical sense. Our life has been different to yours. We live the way crystals live.

WW: Echevit, what tasks do the undines carry out when plants are growing?

The Watery One: We transport life in the plants. We are the life in the plants. Just as the blood circulates in you, so the undines circulate through the plants, forming the leaves and establishing contact with the sylphs, so that through them the light of the sun can shine into the leaves. That's what you call photosynthesis.

WW: Can undines also become fish?

The Watery One: Yes, but they don't have to. They become fish when they want to live.

WW: Who decides whether undines become fish? They don't have any freedom.

The Watery One: The hierarchies decide.

WW: How do the undines bind and loosen substances in the plant kingdom?

The Watery One: If a human being were to do this, he would use his hands, he would bring the substances to the plants where he hands them over. That corresponds to the spiritual task of the world chemists, the undines. The chemical forces still lie in relative obscurity for the human understanding. These chemical forces enable a substance to be partially sublimated and pushed out at another spot. That's similar to how Eknaton carries fire. It's hard to express. The sphere of the chemical forces is still largely a science hidden from humans.

WW: Valliniyu, which music do the sylphs perceive through the flight of the birds?

The Airy One: The music of the spheres.

WW: Is it beautiful music?

The Airy One: It depends. It depends which bird and which sphere it is. It can, for example, screech quite terribly.

WW: Which birds make the most beautiful music?

The Airy One: What's beautiful for you?

WW: Simply describe which birds through their flight make the most pleasant music for you.

The Airy One: The swallows.

WW: What relationship do sylphs have to birds?

The Airy One: We carry them, but we don't like them.

WW: Can sylphs also become birds?

The Airy One: Yes.

WW: And what relationship do sylphs have to plants?

The Airy One: They weave around the plants. They bring the forces of light and hand these over to the undines. This occurs in the leaf and flower spheres.

Verena Staël von Holstein: That's something quite funny, for it looks like they're pulling the flowers out.

WW: Eknaton, what jobs do the salamanders perform in the sphere of the flowers and with the seeds of the plants?

The Fiery One: We weave warmth. That creates fruit. We "minimize" the cosmos into a seed. Every plant is able to embed a large part of the macrocosmos in its microcosmic seed.

WW: What relationship do salamanders have to bees?

The Fiery One: Bees are sun beings. They live with the rhythm of the sun. We don't like them so much. But bees are very important because they're able to weave the light into their honeycombs. That's why the combs are so perfect. Honey can only be produced in these perfect forms. Sometimes we're forced to be bees.

WW: Why don't you like bees? Because you could become bees?

The Fiery One: Yes. Spirit beings always prefer the way they are, and they don't like the other equivalent state if they have to enter into physical existence.

WW: Kapuvu, it's said that gnomes like looking at people when they're falling asleep. What would a person see if he could see the gnomes in a dream during the time he's falling asleep?

The Stone One: The sight would have had an effect like itching powder. The gnomes have then been like ants.

WW: And why do gnomes like looking at people when they're falling asleep?

The Stone One: Because the person has then been a beautiful being. Because it's been beautiful for us stone beings when the human body has come closer to being a stone.

WW: It has less to do with the thoughts which go with a person into the spiritual world when he falls asleep as with his physical body remaining behind in bed, from which the astral body and ego have withdrawn?

The Stone One: That's exactly how it's been.

WW: From the human point of view are there good-natured gnomes and malicious gnomes?

The Stone One: Yes.

WW: Can you describe these a little?

The Stone One: Gnomes also exist who have been both. Gnomes who have been together with cement haven't been good-natured to humans, because they've have had been wrongly put together, so to speak. Because humans have sort of tried to have been a creator but haven't had taken any responsibility. When a gnome has been in natural surroundings, for example, in the Harz region in Germany or in Norway, he's been — except in mining areas — relatively good-natured, because he can have had lived how the upper hierarchies have had imagined for him.

WW: Do malicious gnomes originate just from cement and similar things or in other areas of life as well?

The Stone One: They also originate through other things, but not often. They originate, for example, from pressure in the earth. This happens at many places in mines. Here are spheres where cosmic forces and the forces of stone meet, where an exceptional denseness prevails and malicious gnomes come into being. These gnomes are packed tight together, which makes them unhappy, as a human would have had said.

WW: What effect do these malicious gnomes have on humans?

The Stone One: An unpleasant one.

WW: What can they do?

The Stone One: Cause a human to stumble. They can have built houses badly. They can have radiated negatively out of the walls and out of the human body, they can have softened the bones. They can also have reduced a mind to greed, for this is also a characteristic of gnomes! The hoarding of money and miserliness are also connected to this. The perpetual know-all is also a gnome.

WW: Valliniyu, are there also malicious sylphs?

The Airy One: Yes, polluted air creates malicious sylphs. When industrial plants and high chimneys are situated in the wrong places, vortices are created which can in fact be measured, and these vortices can become very malicious. You humans often have a good feeling for the wind. You speak about the greedy wind and feel the wind eating you up. A wind blowing on a North Sea beach is nice and pleasant even if it's strong. But a wind across an empty car park, where perhaps an empty can is rolling around, is experienced as unpleasant, cold and dead. The wind beings feel exactly the same. We wind beings can be very light and feel everything. We feel everything, please don't forget it!

WW: What effect do malicious sylphs have on people?

The Airy One: They generate malicious thoughts. These are thoughts which have a tendency towards meanness, jealousy and envy.

WW: Echevit, are there also malicious undines?

The Watery One: Yes. They are created through sick water. But they can also arise in some swamps, and they arise between Scylla and Charybdis, in other words through natural whirlpools in the sea. They are created through the crushing movements of the water. This also occurs in the case of ships' turbines. When turbines crush the water malicious undines are generated. Every ship powered with turbines produces malicious undines.

WW: What effect do malicious undines have on humans?

The Watery One: They affect spiritually human emotional and life spheres and produce nasty feelings. They can also produce illnesses. They bring about feelings of frustration, boredom and depression. The malicious undines are active in these feelings of humans.

WW: Eknaton, are there also malicious salamanders?

The Fiery One: Yes. They are created through malicious thoughts, through hatred.

WW: What effect do they have on people?

The Fiery One: Every feeling of hatred is a malevolent salamander. When they become huge, wars arise.

WW: Does a feeling of hate in a human arise through a malicious salamander or do humans produce malicious salamanders through their feelings of hatred?

The Fiery One: It depends where you're looking from. If you look from one direction, the salamander arises out of the hatred, if you look from the other direction, hatred arises out of the salamander.

WW: They're interdeterminate?

The Fiery One: Yes and no. Just as every birth is a new one so is every feeling of hatred. And every salamander is also a new one.

WW: If a malevolent salamander wants to tease hate out of a human, how can the human protect himself?

The Fiery One: Love.

WW: A malicious salamander is warded off through love?

The Fiery One: Yes, it has to withdraw. Love is the best antidote for hate.

WW: Echevit, is it true that undines have a death-wish and want to be eaten as spiritual food by angels and archangels in summer over the Baltic Sea?

The Watery One: Yes, of course.

WW: Can you please explain that in more detail?

The Watery One: Undines are life, consequently their other side is death. That has to be. An undine is always gladly willing to die, because seen spiritually, it's pure life. Life can't exist without death. Eternal life in a physical sense is just human wishful thinking. There's no eternal life on the physical plane. Eternal life is at a higher level. Life and death have to exist, and in fact always simultaneously. If you eradicate death, you'll also eradicate life.

WW: Why do the undines particularly want to be breathed in by higher beings over the Baltic Sea?

The Watery One: I'm not allowed to say.

WW: Just over the Baltic Sea?
The Watery One: No, also over the Sargasso Sea.
WW: Valliniyu, how do sylphs die?
The Airy One: They die in the darkness, in inversion.
VS: It's a difficult question for him, he's not answering it very well.
The Airy One: They die in the transformation of light into darkness.
The death of a sylph is connected to the appearance of darkness.

7. The High One

Wolfgang Weirauch: Hello. Who are you, and what tasks do you have?

The High One: I am a member of the hierarchies. And at the moment I am watching over us.

WW: I've heard it's very hard for humans to talk to you. Why?

The High One: Because my being is hard to endure for humans. I am too direct. My brothers and I gave language to humans. These brothers are the spirits of language. And it's relatively difficult for one human alone to endure us. Every higher spiritual being, every angel, every archangel is terrible.

WW: What relationship do you have to the sun?

The High One: I am the face of the sun. I am the guardian of the sun and the present era.

WW: What relationship do you have to Christ?

The High One: I stand in front of him. Behind me stands Christ.

WW: What relationship do you have to your brothers?

The High One: We pass the cycle of time on amongst us and we confer with one another. I have good contact with a few of my brothers, with others it's much harder. There are many of them, but you humans have only given names to a few of them. It is very difficult with the planetary spirit of Saturn, but you know that. But I can't say everything about that, you wouldn't be able to bear it.

8. The Paper Being

Wolfgang Weirauch: Hello.

The Paper Being: Hello.

WW: What kind of a being are you?

The Paper Being: I'm patience. I'm the being who had to come into existence when humans discovered paper. I carry your information which you commit to paper.

WW: Do you know everything that's written down on every piece of paper?

The Paper Being: Yes, everything!

WW: Good God! Are you responsible for all the paper in the world?

The Paper Being: My higher aspect, yes.

WW: You therefore know the contents of every book?

The Paper Being: Yes. I also know the contents of every slip of paper, every note, every comic, and so on.

WW: When one considers everything that gets written, then it must be horrendous.

The Paper Being: It is horrendous! You said it! Though I also know the Words of God on paper, the Holy Scripture and the Holy Books. They're beautiful.

WW: When was the first paper produced?

The Paper Being: Paper in the broadest sense of the word in ancient Egypt.

WW: Do you also then carry the writings on papyrus?

The Paper Being: Yes. Basically I also represent animal skins and similar materials used for writing; these were the preliminary stages of paper. I am responsible from the moment information is written down. My being is information which has been physically fixed.

WW: What happens when a human takes a piece of paper and writes on it?

The Paper Being: He doesn't just write on the paper but also in the world ether. And that can never be erased. There are lunatics who instigate the burning of books in order to erase the content of these books. But in doing so they do the opposite. The content of these books is then written with fire into the world ether.

WW: You mean the Nazis.

The Paper Being: Yes, but not only them, Christian monks too, the Taliban and many others have done it. The Christians burned many books in Arab lands. The contents of these books cannot now be read by humans, but they've been burned into the world ether.

WW: Judging from everything you've said, you prefer living in libraries.

The Paper Being: En masse.

WW: Are you *one* being, or do you have many deputies?

The Paper Being: I am *one* being and I am *very many* beings. An aspect of my being is connected with every book but they aren't deputies like house spirits have. Paper is interconnected, all paper is in effect *one* paper. It's just divided up into countless pieces. To a certain extent I'm also responsible for digital data recording, although not completely, but I'm also not completely uninvolved.

WW: What's the difference between a book with a beautiful content and one with an ugly content?

The Paper Being: That's quite easy, every child knows the answer to that. When it opens a book which it likes, it meets its friends. When on the other hand it opens a book that's bad and which it does't like, then it meets its enemies. There are worlds in paper.

WW: Is a bad book for you like a cancerous growth for a human?

The Paper Being: Roughly speaking. According to how bad it is, it can get to be like a cancerous growth.

WW: Do you know the beings who are called the Fools?

The Paper Being: The ones you like to collect around you so much?

WW: What kind of beings are they?

The Paper Being: They're the lead weights for thoughts. They whir around intelligent humans and feed on clever words and thoughts.

WW: And why do I like to collect these beings around me?

The Paper Being: Because you like to think and express clever thoughts. Each one of these Fools, these beings of stupidity, gives a clever thought stability. A condition of balance has to be achieved. The Fools are hungry for clever thoughts and they eat them up.

WW: Is it a good thing having such beings around one?

The Paper Being: It's good for the world.

WW: Is it true these beings also live in cemeteries?

The Paper Being: Yes, near the graves of clever humans. The Fools a human has gathered around him during his life, are there where his corpse is buried.

WW: Are these Fools necessary in terms of energy if one wants to form a thought?

The Paper Being: The beam of a weighing scale always has two ends.

WW: Do humans with stupid thoughts have such Fools around them?

The Paper Being: No. They're Fools enough in themselves.

WW: Can you also say something about the beings of ugliness, who exist so that an artist can create a beautiful work of art?

The Paper Being: That's not my field. Ask the Glass One. He's more beautiful than me.

WW: Little Glass Man, can you come?

Little Glass Man: You have to give me a name for today first.

WW: Why?

Verena Staël von Holstein: The Little Glass Man is given a new name every day. Otherwise he gets touchy.

WW: Can it be a human name as well?

VS: Any old name.

WW: Then I'll call you Gamila.

Little Glass Man: Excellent, that's a lovely name.

WW: It's a woman's name though, and it means "beautiful" in Arabic. Can you tell me something about the beings of ugliness, who are necessary for the creation of beautiful art?

Little Glass Man: You humans have to try and understand these connections. In almost every respect, you humans are the point of balance on which the weighing scales rest. That's your being. You decide if you want to turn more to Lucifer or to Ahriman. You have to try and keep centred. Your whole experience is about staying centred. When you see beauty, ugliness has to be there. Beauty cannot exist without ugliness. It's *still* the case that the one can't be present without its opposite. When you create beauty the beings of ugliness eat it and the beauty becomes even more beautiful in the process. That's vitally important. That's how it is almost everywhere.

WW: So a beautiful work of art is surrounded by these beings of ugliness.

Little Glass Man: Yes. And the ugliness is offset in the process. The work of art created by humans compensates for the ugliness.

WW: And when a work of art is ugly, what then?

Little Glass Man: Then humans have until the end of the world to create a being of beauty which can balance out this ugly work of art. Here the element of time comes into consideration. A work doesn't have to be compensated for at the same time as it's created.

WW: Paper Being, what happens when paper is manufactured? Is that a process in which you're also involved?

The Paper Being: Yes and no. There's an awful lot of paper produced. I spread myself out when paper is manufactured. That's quite boring.

WW: What happens when paper is ripped?

The Paper Being: It's like you having your hair cut.

WW: There are different kinds of paper. Is it a matter of indifference to you out of which material paper is manufactured?

The Paper Being: No, it's not at all a matter of indifference. Paper is my being, but for the information on the paper, it's unimportant. For me though it's my body, just like you have a physical body. I would of course prefer to be manufactured from wholesome material. I like being beautiful as well, I like also being handmade paper. I'm not so keen about being toilet paper.

WW: Thank you for the conversation.

The Paper Being: You're welcome.

WW: In your book you describe how all of a sudden you discovered the Grey Creeper. Can you describe this event once more?

VS: I discovered him one morning as I was walking from the house to the barn, some thirty odd metres. And I saw how he was walking over the meadow. The Grey Creeper is quite a sad being, and looks somewhat like a bent-over telegraph mast with a grey cloak. The meeting was rather horrible. Then I asked my friends what kind of a being it was. And they said it was a drought being. That was in the spring of 2000, and soon afterwards in May a period of drought set in, which came too early for many plants. There was much damage to the plants because of this period of drought. That was an exciting event, first perceiving this drought being and later actually experiencing a drought.

WW: What astonishes me about it is that you first perceived this Grey Creeper being, and not the nature-beings, especially not those responsible for the water balance and the plants.

VS: In some respects nature-beings see no further than their own noses. They don't have the all-round vision human beings have. They also don't have the extensive curiosity of human beings, they don't take an interest in everything. They're experts in their fields and are also curious when it comes to something in their field but they don't notice everything. The nature-beings were astonished that the Grey Creeper came so early. They hadn't reckoned with him, at least not so early.

WW: Were the nature-beings grateful as you pointed out the presence of the Grey Creeper to them?

VS: Yes.

WW: Miller, can you explain a little the significance of the Grey Creeper?

Miller: The Grey Creeper is used by the creators of the weather, and these weather makers see the necessity of causing disruption through drought.

WW: How do the other nature-beings feel about this Grey Creeper?

Miller: The Green Ones are very afraid of the Grey Creeper, because the plants are their charges. The Watery One also fears him, but he's old enough and knows he's already survived many periods of drought. The Grey Creeper hardly affects me as a house being.

WW: When there's a period of drought, do many Grey Creepers come or just the one?

Miller: It's just like all nature-beings. There's a pyramid of Grey Creepers with one being at the top. My human saw *one* Grey Creeper.

WW: Gnunno, can you say how these Grey Creepers get their nourishment?

The Green One: They get nourishment above all from humans seeing sunny weather as the best, the most fantastic and most praiseworthy weather, and from them calling it lovely weather. Damp and rainy weather on the other hand they call bad weather. In spring humans demand from nature that she should blossom and grow but they still want the weather to remain dry and sunny. That's an absurdity. Beings of drought are created much more easily through such distorted notions.

WW: They're created by human thoughts as well?

The Green One: Yes, they're also created by the thoughts and wishes of humans. Such beings are strongly influenced especially by humans dividing the weather into good and bad. Rain is bad weather, sun is good weather. But this doesn't correspond at all to the way of life of we nature spirits.

WW: Do such drought beings arise in a solarium?

The Green One: Very small ones, yes.

WW: Do you as a plant being fight these drought beings?

The Green One: Yes and no. We try to protect our charges. That's a bit different from actively fighting. We're not free.

WW: How do you protect the plants from the drought beings?

The Green One: By trying with the Watery One and all water beings to bring more water. We try to give water to the plants, even the smallest amounts.

WW: Echevit, can you say more about the tasks of a drought being?

The Watery One: The drought beings don't want to be seen. They draw the life energy out of the water. And in the process draw life energy out of the earth. This is connected to humans forming false conceptions of life.

WW: Why do the drought beings not want to be seen?

The Watery One: To paraphrase George Lucas, because they belong to the dark side of power. Knowledge damages these beings. Bring light into darkness, and the darkness vanishes.

WW: Do these drought beings want the earth to die?

The Watery One: The question is wrongly formulated. They wouldn't stop the earth dying. But it's not their intention to let something die. They're beings of drought and that's why they see what they do as being justified.

WW: But where something dies are these beings of drought there?

The Watery One: Yes, but only when it's a dry death. If someone drowns you won't experience a drought being.

WW: How powerful are these beings in a desert, for example, in the Sahara?

The Watery One: There they dominate.

WW: Are they huge beings?

The Watery One: There are many beings, they're not huge. Beings of warmth — and drought beings belong here — are more on the small side, but they're powerful. That's no contradiction, for even something small can be powerful.

WW: What relationship do the drought beings in a desert have to a person traveling through the desert?

The Watery One: He's of no interest to them. But if someone doesn't know his way around particularly well in the desert, he won't survive the drought. Though the drought beings aren't interested in killing.

WW: To which grouping of nature-beings do the drought beings belong?

The Watery One: They're not demons. They belong to the Grey Beings. Drought beings are also necessary. At present, during a wet, late summer, many farmers would welcome the drought beings.

WW: And would you let them come now as well?

The Watery One: We don't decide that. We're not free.

WW: Can human beings help to create a harmonious balance between water beings and drought beings?

The Watery One: Yes, if they could finally pull themselves together and understand the weather as harmonious and to praise the rain, when it falls in moderate amounts, just as much as the sun when it moderately shines. Humans would be helping nature a lot with that. Each and every human should develop an awareness here. Any term expressing merely personal value judgments should be left out when speaking about the weather. To speak about bad weather just because you're going to get wet in a shower of rain is totally uncalled-for.

9. Evil

Wolfgang Weirauch: What are demons?

The Watery One: Demons are beings of the descending powers out of the dark regions, who are caused amongst other things by people's lies. They also arise through wrong human thoughts. Just as we're children of the angels, so are demons children or pieces split-off from the fallen angels.

WW: Does every lie spoken by a human create a demon of lies?

The Watery One: Certainly. And if it's a white lie, it's a little demon, if on the other hand it's a serious lie, a huge demon is created.

WW: What do these demons of lies do in the world after they've been created?

The Watery One: They roam around destroying what they can. They destroy good thoughts and work against the ascending elements of world evolution. They try and destabilize the equilibrium in favour of the powers of evil.

WW: Can these demons of lies so influence humans that they'll also tell new lies.

The Watery One: Yes, of course. They can even become so big and strong that they possess humans. Throughout history and in Bible stories there were casting-out of demons, and they are to be taken quite literally.

WW: When Christ drove demons out of humans, they fled, for example, into swine. Is that a correct description?

The Watery One: That's something that's not necessarily desirable. Ask the Brown One. But it's conceivable. Swine anyway have the tendency to root around in filth, and so basically represent symbolically the mendacious side of humans.

WW: If a group of people tells lots of lies over a certain period of time do the demons of lies they've created then stay in the vicinity of this group?

The Watery One: If a group of people tells lies, or dedicates itself to certain lies, larger demons get created. These beings are called spectres. If these spectres can't be treated with positive thoughts by the group of people they'll return again and again to the group, and they'll meet the people after their death as well and even at their next birth.

WW: Assuming a demon of lies or a spectre has been created, how can they be eliminated?

The Watery One: If you've accidently lied then it helps to admit it straight away. If after such a lie you add a good thought then things get evened out, and the demon of lies dissolves away. It's much more difficult in the case of spectres, because it's very hard to bring a group of people to take a similar positive point of view. That's why spectres are much harder to dissolve. Human beings are free, and when on one day a group of people creates a spectre through a lie, it's difficult for the free human beings to meet again on the next day under different circumstances. But if a few people from this group make the effort, positive beings can also be created who then commence battle with the spectres. The spectres and the struggles with them burden the earth's karma, the total sphere of the earth, and at present there are many such struggles, which also produce thunderstorms. The Hosts of Michael are participating on the good side in these struggles.

WW: I know a group in which over a certain period very many lies were told which to a large extent have not been corrected. But because this was many years ago, other people have joined this group who have nothing to do with these lies. How can the people who have since joined protect themselves from the demons of lies and spectres buzzing around this group?

The Watery One: They have to leave the group.

WW: And if that's not possible.

The Watery One: There is no other way. Otherwise these people will have to carry the burden of the group in their karma.

WW: Are there any individual defence mechanisms to protect one against demons of lies?

The Watery One: Praying.

WW: Can you say something about the human *doppelgänger*? What kind of a being is it?

The Watery One: No, I'm not an angel.

WW: Only the High One can talk about that?

The Watery One: Yes,

WW: What happens spiritually during an eclipse of the sun?

The Watery One: That's a good question. In the shadow which move across the earth during an eclipse of the sun, powerful forces of destruction flow in because at that moment Christ isn't looking.

WW: Can evil cosmic forces stream on to the earth at that moment?

The Watery One: Yes.

WW: Did this also happen during the 1999 eclipse of the sun?

The Watery One: Yes.

WW: Do these forces flowing in affect individuals or the whole of mankind?

The Watery One: Both the one as well as the other. Every hole during a solar eclipse can be occupied. Every hollow space you've created in the earth can be filled at such a moment with huge negative beings.

WW: Can you speak about the Other Ones and the Sun Demon. What kind of beings are they?

The Watery One: The Other Ones is a general term for demons, spectres, drought beings, in other words all the smaller spirit beings from the grey and the dark side. All smaller nature-beings are afraid of the great Sun Demon, and are afraid of saying his name. Only we larger beings can endure his name.

WW: What's the task of the Sun Demon?

The Watery One: He hinders the effectiveness of Christ.

WW: How does he get nourishment?

The Watery One: From black magic, from lack of faith, from hatred, from dark thoughts, and from ingrained materialism. Materialism makes him really fat.

WW: Can he also flow into people who think accordingly?

The Watery One: Yes, and he steers or incites them to actions.

Although at present he's still being very careful so as not to make too obvious an appearance. He's also not quite completely here. But his power will increase. You should say his name as little as possible if the room is not filled with prayers.

WW: Why should the name of the Sun Demon not be spoken?

The Watery One: Names incarnate. Writing and reading are possible, but the name should not be *spoken.*

WW: What kind of a being is Lucifer?

The Watery One: He's a very beautiful being and was at one time a higher angel. He's a powerful being.

WW: Is he the most beautiful being in the cosmos?

The Watery One: That's quite a difficult way of formulating it. No, I wouldn't put it that way. For me as a water being something else is beautiful.

WW: What tasks does Lucifer have?

The Watery One: To enthuse humans and make them progress. But he's always trying to do everything too soon. Lucifer inspires and brings things to mankind which leads them on. He brings important things from out of the spiritual world and transforms them to human abilities. When seen in this light he's very helpful to mankind. Through their deeds, the powers of evil are making a great sacrifice in the background. This aspect of theirs has always to be kept in mind. But that doesn't mean finding everything the powers of evil achieve good.

WW: Do humans have the task of one day redeeming these powers of evil?

The Watery One: Yes.

WW: Will they succeed?

The Watery One: That I don't know.

WW: What kind of a being is Ahriman?

The Watery One: He's cold, he's cold as a CD. And he's extremely clever. He's brilliant, but not inspiring. He's much cleverer than you can imagine. But he's ugly.

WW: What does he look like then?

The Watery One: There's a beautiful statue carved by Rudolf

Steiner, which represents him the best. He has a long chin and a high forehead and wears glasses.

WW: Why does he wear glasses?

The Watery One: At present he's wearing glasses.

WW: Why's Ahriman at present wearing glasses?

The Watery One: Because that corresponds to the picture of himself he wishes to convey to present-day humans. But he operates very much in secret, completely in contrast to Lucifer. That's one of the most interesting differences between the two of them. The one likes to take centre stage, while the other one hides himself as much as possible.

WW: Ahriman hates being recognized.

The Watery One: Exactly.

WW: Is it a form of defence against Ahriman if you know how Ahriman operates and what the character traits of his being are?

The Watery One: You're all still not strong enough to protect yourselves from Ahriman. For that you'll have to get to know yourselves a lot better. Know yourself — that will best protect you from him.

WW: Is there a part of every single human which Ahriman has taken over?

The Watery One: At present, yes. That has to be.

WW: What necessary tasks does Ahriman have?

The Watery One: He forms the counterweight to Lucifer, which is the most necessary thing there ever could be. He fixes matter and prevents the earth from turning into a fireball. Matter can only exist through both being in balance.

WW: What kind of beings are the Asuras?

The Watery One: They come from another world.

WW: Can this world be described?

The Watery One: No, I'm not allowed to. It's a world beyond our cosmos.

WW: And what effect do the Asuras have here in our world?

The Watery One: Like cancer. They devour a part of the self.

WW: How does the human open himself to these beings?

The Watery One: The Asuras are beings from beyond the cosmos. When they come, they come more in the form of external attacks.

WW: Can humans not protect themselves from these attacks?

The Watery One: Not very easily. Humans don't invite them, as they have to in relation to Ahriman and Lucifer. They come without being invited.

WW: When do they come in particular?

The Watery One: They're coming more and more often, but their effect isn't yet so strong. It'll get worse in the future.

WW: But there must surely be some kind of protection, with which humans can ward these Asuras off.

The Watery One: A human can always pray and entrust himself to the leadership of the good spiritual beings. This he does by carrying his karma in a Christian way. It's also important that he's content with his life, for discontent makes him open to attack.

WW: Do the Asuras have anything to do with Ahriman?

The Watery One: No, they're completely independent.

WW: To which hierarchy do they belong?

The Watery One: To absolutely none.

WW: What takes place during a black mass?

The Watery One: Demons, spectres and phantoms are attracted and integrated into the black mass. In addition the hosts of fallen angels are addressed and integrated into the congregation present. Or a being is taken over willingly or unwillingly in a black mass. In this connection there are various forms of black masses, new and old.

WW: Are there nowadays still any black magicians?

The Watery One: Yes.

WW: Many?

The Watery One: What does many mean? Too many!

WW: Do all black magicians know what they're doing?

The Watery One: There are a few who play around. And then there are many who are initiated into the black path.

10. The Cycle of the Year and Christian Festivals

Wolfgang Weirauch: What happens in the cosmos and on the earth on Maundy Thursday?

The Watery One: On which Maundy Thursday? On the original one or on every one?

WW: On every one.

The Watery One: It's the day of the beginning of the Eucharist, on this day the Church communities were created and this is renewed every year on this day. For us nature-beings this day signifies that the angels concern themselves in a specially intensive way with the Church communities.

WW: Is this day different in nature?

The Watery One: On Maundy Thursday we prepare ourselves for waiting.

WW: What happens on Good Friday cosmically and on the earth?

The Watery One: On Good Friday everything stands still, nature holds its breath. That's quite a horrible pause. We nature-beings don't know — even me as a nix — whether this year Easter will come again.

WW: You mean it could happen that one year Easter doesn't come?

The Watery One: Yes, we hold our breaths. Everything stands still, nothing moves or does anything at all. Quite serious damage is done to the world if the silence of Good Friday and Easter Saturday is disturbed. On this day the world is dead.

WW: The whole of Good Friday?

The Watery One: From midday, and it lasts until the moment the Easter sun rises.

WW: How can the silence of Good Friday be disturbed?

The Watery One: Through various activities, above all through humans not knowing what this day means. On this day you shouldn't kill or prepare any meat. You shouldn't let any blood flow. You shouldn't perform any operation, not damage the surface of the earth and not cut any plants.

WW: Do the nature-beings have any special tasks during the time of Lent?

The Watery One: Yes, we're preparing for the new birth. Lent is always in spring. There are reasons for that. Lent isn't in autumn, and people should give a lot more thought to why Lent is in spring and not in the dark time of the year.

WW: It's actually quite a contrast.

The Watery One: It's *not* a contrast. But you don't understand that yet.

WW: In outer nature something grows and is resurrected, in inner nature something dies.

The Watery One: In a certain way every Good Friday corresponds to an eclipse of the sun. And there was indeed an eclipse of the sun on the real Good Friday.

WW: Does the process of Christ's death recur every Good Friday?

The Watery One: Yes, every Good Friday.

WW: How do you nature-beings experience this death process?

The Watery One: As extremely painful. The whole of nature suffers on this day.

WW: How can humans help you during this?

The Watery One: By staying calm, by thinking, sympathizing and suffering together with us. Practise compassion!

WW: So you do know what compassion is!

The Watery One: Humans experience compassion, not us. We know though what compassion is, but we can't experience it ourselves. You know as well what spirit is, and nevertheless can't create it.

WW: Do rituals help in this period?

The Watery One: Yes, of course. Experiencing the processes of nature in connection with ritual is very important in keeping the earth healthy. The more this connection disappears from the earth the sooner will the earth become sclerotic and sick.

WW: Can you describe what happens in nature on Easter Sunday?

The Watery One: It rejoices. It rejoices, whether it's raining or not. Usually the sun shines on Easter Sunday at least for a while. Nature simply rejoices, it's delighted, there's an enormous beauty. We all sing and dance with one another. Stones dance with fire, fire dances with water. We celebrate the renewal of the world. This world would no longer exist without Easter. And that's how it is every Easter Sunday.

WW: How long do you celebrate? One day, forty days or fifty days?

The Watery One: Until Ascension Day, that's forty days.

WW: What do the nature spirits do on Walpurgis Night?*

The Watery One: The nature spirits dance on this day too but we're joined by human spirits. It's the day of the witches, actually a very old ritual, relating to sexuality. On this day the male principle unites with the female principle — something new is created. Only in a higher sense of course, does this have any meaning for us.

WW: Is this day beautiful for you?

The Watery One: Unfortunately recently it has become very distorted. What is important for this day is the idea of union, the basic principle of procreation. The female principle unites with the male principle. That ancient cultures celebrated this day by practising procreation in the flesh was right. It would also do the world good today if humans did it on this day — combined with higher awareness.

WW: What does Ascension mean for humans and the earth?

The Watery One: Ascension is now, we're living in the age of the Ascension. Ascension means that Christ has united himself with the etheric sphere of the earth. For we etheric beings that's something a bit like how Easter is for you. For us it's a kind of resurrection. And the resurrection in the etheric world is now tangible. The etheric Christ is walking now with us in the etheric world.

WW: Who is the Holy Spirit, and what tasks does he have at Whitsun?

* The night before May 1 when German folklore tells of witches flying to their dancing place.

The Watery One: It's not my responsibility to speak about it. My competence as a water being ends here.

WW: Can you nevertheless say what happens in nature at Whitsun?

The Watery One: Whitsun is joy and healing in nature. The side of Whitsun which we nature-beings understand, is the activity of the healing spirit. It's spontaneous healing from the higher realms of the world.

WW: In other words healing forces come streaming into nature?

The Watery One: Yes. Many scars caused by humans and the Other Ones are healed in this period.

WW: What happens in nature on St John's Day?

The Watery One: At St John's tide the crystallization of the cosmic forces in the earth begins.

WW: Do you celebrate this day?

The Watery One: Yes. In addition we give our best forces to the crystals.

WW: What does Michaelmas mean for the nature-beings and for the earth?

The Watery One: At Michaelmas the earth begins to give light back to the sun. The resurrection of the earth is beginning to be prepared. The leaves become golden and shine back. And this process ends at Christmas.

WW: What about Advent?

The Watery One: Advent is pregnancy, the heavens open.

WW: Is it true then that the angels during Advent are looking down at the earth?

The Watery One: Yes.

WW: Is that why humans are so restless?

The Watery One: They should actually be calm. Only those who have no belief become restless. They sense the closeness of the angels and this they experience as a disturbing contradiction to their lives.

WW: What does Christmas mean for nature?

The Watery One: That's the twelve Holy Days and the thirteen Holy Nights. Never forget there are *thirteen* Holy Nights! The first is the night from December 24 to 25, and the last night is that ending on January 6.

WW: What happens to nature during these days and nights?

The Watery One: During this period nature directly receives the cosmic forces. Heaven is then wide open, and humans should have prepared themselves to such an extent that on these twelve days and thirteen nights they do nothing, at most just meditating. At least that would be the best state to be in. But that isn't possible over the course of a normal human day. The hierarchies manifest themselves in the world during these days, always one for one day or night. That's why it has to be thirteen.

WW: But there are only nine hierarchies of angels, or how is that to be understood?

The Watery One: The mineral kingdom, the plant kingdom, the animal kingdom, humans and the nine hierarchies of angels. Actually above the hierarchies of angels are more, but they're far away, which is why they play no part.

WW: And each of these thirteen hierarchies has its special night?

The Watery One: That's right. The night from December 24 to 25 is the night of the mineral kingdom, because Christ has arrived in the earth. And then comes the night of the plants, the night of the animals, and so on.

WW: Does New Year have any special meaning?

The Watery One: Yes, New Year lies in the middle of the twelve Holy Days and the thirteen Holy Nights and also divides the years. It's a very important day. It's the day for looking back.

WW: On this day humans should take a look back?

The Watery One: Definitely.

WW: Does New Year also have any meaning for nature?

The Watery One: Only a secondary one. Nature doesn't look back. It's unnecessary!

WW: What does Epiphany mean?

The Watery One: That's the day of the birth of the second Jesus child, whose story is told in the Gospel of Matthew. But you know that! Even if unfortunately most humans no longer know it. This Jesus child is the future one.

WW: What meaning does this day have for nature?

The Watery One: The same as December 25. In the night of December 25 the Jesus everyone knows was born, the past one. His birth is described in the Gospel of Luke. Humans should actually celebrate Christmas on January 6. Because the King's son is now the more important one. We've convinced our humans to celebrate Christmas on January 6.

WW: Many thanks for your explanations.

The Watery One: You're welcome.

Verena Staël von Holstein: Echevit didn't put it so clearly but it's very important for the nature-beings that humans become aware of the other half of Christmas. Most people pack their Christmas things away at New Year. And it's one terrible effect of the Ahrimanic beings that the Matthew Jesus has been forgotten. The Matthew Jesus is connected to knowledge, while the Luke Jesus is connected to feeling and is often sentimentalized by people. He's made mawkish. The nature-beings think that's quite dreadful. They're for ever emphasizing that we have to remember the future, the cosmic, the knowing Jesus and Christ. He's the bearer of wisdom and not of feeling.

11. Kollii, the One from the Marsh

Verena Staël von Holstein: You're looking muddy.
Wolfgang Weirauch: Hello.
Kollii, The One from the Marsh: Hello.
WW: Why do you look so muddy?
Kollii: Because I was just down in the marsh.
WW: What have you just done there?
Kollii: I opened a new water channel. There's enough water in the river valley at present, and that's why we're laying new water channels.
WW: Can you describe your being?
Kollii: I'm a being of permanence and of the marsh woodlands here. My activity extends over an area with a radius of approximately fifty kilometres.
WW: How old are you?
Kollii: I exist since the marsh woods have been here. They arose after the last Ice Age. I'm somewhat younger than the Watery One, because he was here before me.
WW: Were you born, or how did you come into existence?
Kollii: I was born, because I'm a marsh spirit. And the marsh gives birth to itself.
WW: Can you describe this process?
Kollii: An especially large bubble filled with marsh gas had formed and I was extracted out of this. I'm relatively akin to you humans.
WW: To what extent?
Kollii: My form is similar to the human form, and my behaviour is likewise fairly similar. The gnomes, the Green Ones and the tree spirits are mixed into my being. In the former Nordic culture we were very important. This tradition has unfortunately become submerged, but it will come again. The people living here should contemplate that this region belongs to the

Nordic culture, not the humanist culture. In former times people went to the marsh, to pronounce judgment because they knew that here the forces of growth and decay are active, the eternal process of transformation, which gives birth to life and death.

WW: What did those people do at such a trial?

Kollii: The elders — who were not necessarily biologically the oldest, but the oldest souls — pronounced judgment. (A child could also number among these elders; a child could also be head of a tribe if it was born on December 25.) Those who were judged were pushed into the marsh, and whoever was innocent survived this process. People who, for example, had committed adultery or theft were sat upon in judgment.

WW: And when someone was innocent did you protect him?

Kollii: Exactly. And when he was guilty he became a will-o'-the-wisp.

WW: What are will-o'-the-wisps?

Kollii: Wandering souls expelled from the tribal bonds of the time and pushed into the marsh. They carry on living in the marsh after they've physically died there.

WW: Do any will-o'-the-wisps still live in the marsh nowadays?

Kollii: Yes.

WW: Are they the humans who died in the marsh from the period you've just talked about?

Kollii: Not necessarily, for a will-o'-the-wisp can cease flitting about after some thousand years. The punishment for the humans in such cases lies in the fact that they miss possibilities for incarnation.

WW: Because they cannot incarnate themselves as long as they're still will-o'-the.wisps?

Kollii: Exactly. Only when the will-o'-the-wisp has dissolved can the human incarnate again.

WW: Does the self detach itself from that part of the human that's darting over the marsh as a will-o'-the-wisp?

Kollii: The self isn't in the sphere of the will-o'-the-wisp, nevertheless it isn't completely detached from it. It's connected to it as though by a thin wire and that's why it can't achieve a new birth in a physical body on the earth. The marsh conserves.

WW: How can a new relationship to the Nordic gods be created?

Kollii: By praying. The Nordic gods correspond to angels. This should be common knowledge but isn't any more. You should be aware that an Odin, a Thor, a Frey and a Nerthus are walking around here. They belong here and not Venus and Jupiter.

WW: We have a troubled relationship to these gods because of the Nazis.

Kollii: During the Nazi period there was a heavy infiltration of dark beings. And that's exactly why the relationship to the Nordic gods should now be taken up consciously. It was difficult under the being that was called up by the Nazis.

WW: What kind of a being was that?

Kollii: It was a phantom.

WW: Can you describe this being in more detail?

Kollii: I'm not allowed to, I'm not big enough for that.

WW: Can you tell us what responsibilities you have in the marsh?

Kollii: I preserve the process of development and birth in the marsh. I now have to do what humans formerly did. It never harmed the marsh having branches cut from the willows growing in it, quite the reverse. But nobody cuts willow in the marsh anymore. But that would do it good. Nevertheless I try on a small scale to maintain a marsh. There's a lot of work involved in it for me.

Meanwhile a major task of mine is the care of the beings from the towns who have been made sick by humans. The sick nature-beings from the towns or industrial regions are missing some parts. Relating it symbolically to your bodies, they haven't for example got a head or a heart anymore, or they're completely transparent or they've got holes. For them I make marsh-packs, and then they're healed. Because the forces of life in the marsh are very, very strong.

WW: And then the nature-beings return to their original homes?

Kollii: Yes, but they don't like returning to the town. But because they're not free, they have to return. Like all of us they actually like performing their tasks, but humans make it hard for them.

WW: Which beings come as sick nature-beings to you?

Kollii: Plant beings, but mainly tree beings, for they are the worst affected. They come mainly from Hamburg.

WW: What can people do for the tree beings in towns so that they don't get so sick?

Kollii: Make the air healthier. You can choose a tree in the town and say, "Good morning," to it every day. That'll help the tree a lot. You should do it at least once a week. When it's very hot you can also bring it a bucket of water. In this way you can start a tree sponsorship programme. Something like this exists here and there, and such initiatives are very important for tree beings. But the sponsorship then has to be kept up and that causes difficulties for most humans.

WW: Can you describe what your ideal marsh looks like?

Kollii: Why should I describe it? Go outside and take a look yourself. It's there outside.

WW: The people reading our book can't do that.

Kollii: Take a photo. But I'll make the effort. It's a wood, with wet ground, which is marshy and in which black alder, willows, bird cherry, and creepers grow. This marsh contains reeds, flowers in spring, floods in autumn, a wood that's simply fantastic! My humans were with me in the marsh at the last eclipse of the moon. That was very nice.

VS: That was quite a peculiar atmosphere especially being invited by such a nature-being. To be present at an eclipse of the moon in a marsh is an incredible experience.

WW: What happens to the nature-beings at an eclipse of the moon?

Kollii: The past disappears. When the moon is hidden by the earth from the sun being, at the place where the eclipse is, the past is no more.

WW: What does that mean?

Kollii: The place is different when the eclipse is over.

WW: How is something from the past erased during an eclipse of the moon?

Kollii: Not erased, but changed.

WW: Can you give an example?

The marsh

Kollii: They're very difficult examples for you humans. At an eclipse of the moon, for example, the process of decaying is changed just a tiny fraction. These are microcosmic changes arising from a macrocosmic influence. You understand too little of the processes in marshland, and your readers too will understand little of these processes of decay.

WW: Do you also have a refuge?

Kollii: Yes. It's not in the marsh but here in the mill. I'm Miller's friend. Miller and I have been living here a long time, and we have the same tree being as friend.

WW: Thank you very much.

Kollii: You're welcome.

12. Moonlight, the Silver One

Wolfgang Weirauch: Hello.

The Silver One: Always be good to the moonlight.

WW: What do you mean by that?

The Silver One: I am the moonlight.

WW: Can you describe your being in a little more detail?

The Silver One: I'm the personal aspect of silver. Silver corresponds to a cosmic power. Silver is a planetary essence which expresses itself in the earth. There would be no past for the earth without the forces of silver.

WW: Does silver preserve the past?

The Silver One: Silver reflects light and conducts warmth and through this the past can be preserved and well-loved.

WW: Where is your home?

The Silver One: I come from the Harz region. There were silver mines there in former times. And now I'm living in the cellar of the mill along with the other nature-beings.

WW: And will you be staying here for always?

The Silver One: I've committed myself to keeping an eye on a few things here.

WW: And how did you get here?

The Silver One: Through the earth. I travel through the metal, and when there's no metal then we build a silver bridge.

WW: What is a silver bridge like?

The Silver One: It's a rainbow made from etheric silver, and I can then fly from one place to the next across this silver bridge.

WW: Can you describe yourself for those people who can't perceive you?

The Silver One: Have you ever seen a filigree minaret of a mosque?

WW: Yes.

The Silver One: Imagine it made out of silver and even more filigree. That's what I look like. I look like the minaret of a mosque made of spun silver.

WW: Have you left the silver mine in the Harz all to itself?

The Silver One: Yes and no. It's now protected by my mirror. That's my *doppelgänger.* I have a double. Although we're now slowly starting to grow away from one another.

WW: And the only reason this *doppelgänger* being of yours came into being is because you came here to the mill?

The Silver One: Yes. It wasn't there before.

WW: How can we understand the process involved in the creation of a *doppelgänger* being? Do you have to consult with higher beings about this doubling of your being?

The Silver One: The High One did it. He asked me if I was prepared to do it. And in this case such a question is already the answer — he wouldn't have asked if I wasn't ready.

WW: Can you please describe your tasks a little?

The Silver One: I spin a silver net around the being I'm protecting so it can carry on with its activities as undisturbed as possible.

WW: Is it a protection against demons?

The Silver One: Mainly against spectres not demons. Demons are too fine and can slip through such a net. It's like a kitchen sieve. Fine sand trickles through a sieve.

WW: Can you describe the spectres a little?

The Silver One: Spectres are the counterbeings to human group-souls.

WW: How do spectres come into being?

The Silver One: Through institutions or single groups behaving badly. There are small and large spectres. When a state makes unfair decisions a large spectre immediately comes into being.

WW: Through bad laws as well?

The Silver One: Definitely.

WW: Can you give an example?

The Silver One: All unjust laws. The law concerning the return of land in the former East Germany is a totally bad law. Very many spectres have been produced in the process. The sense of justice of the nature-beings involved was wounded by it.

Each single case should have been individually considered. There are humans who lived in the houses of the old German Democratic Republic, who were quite bad for the houses and the respective localities, and there are humans who didn't live there, but who remained faithful to the place. These different relationships ought to have been categorized and could have been as well, although it's difficult. Decisions would have to have been made based on individual cases, using your legal terms.

WW: Do you have another example of a bad law?

The Silver One: The present German divorce law is in my eyes bad, and specifically because custody for the children is shared. The decision relating to the children should be final. They should only live with one of the two marriage partners.

WW: Do you also have an example for a good law?

The Silver One: Almost every law has rough edges, but there are also good laws. Laws reducing car emissions are very good. They just don't go far enough. The laws in Europe gradually making the borders superfluous are very important and good as well, and create a lot of space for good group souls. It's always good when humans develop a common awareness of responsibilities.

WW: Are you familiar with laws in other countries?

The Silver One: Yes, of course. I am silver.

WW: What are your views on the Sharia in Islamic countries?

The Silver One: That's an age old system of justice, whose laws no longer apply to the condition of present-day humans.

WW: Will these laws change?

The Silver One: They will have to change. And when humans aren't capable of doing it alone they'll be forced to do it. It's now the High One's time.

WW: Spectres are caused by bad laws but the beings caused by good laws aren't yet quite clear to me. What kind of beings are they?

The Silver One: They are spaces with which higher spiritual beings can connect. They are group beings for whom my human hasn't any reasonable names. Good and higher spiritual beings superior to humans, connect with these spaces but they're not angels.

WW: Are they harmonious elemental beings?

The Silver One: Yes, this term fits.

WW: What secrets do the metal beings preserve?

The Silver One: Silver is the spiritual knife and preserves the past. We can separate you from your spiritual roots.

WW: Does that mean you could sever a human from his karma?

The Silver One: Yes, that as well.

WW: Is it done sometimes?

The Silver One: Black magicians like to do it. Sometimes it's also necessary to dissolve the smallest parts of someone's karma for a good purpose, in order, for example, to cut a mother-child relationship that's grown too old. Every old connection for which an urgently necessary solution is on the cards, can be cut with a silver knife. Images of ancient Druids cutting with a silver knife are very real.

WW: Who gives you the instructions for cutting someone's karma like that?

The Silver One: Human initiates and the High One helps in the process. Black magicians of course, don't call on the High One, but his counterpart.

WW: What tasks do metals have for the cosmos?

The Silver One: They reflect the cosmic forces in the earth, and these reflected forces radiate into the earth. Bear in mind that you alter the silver of the moon when you send a space probe to the moon. This alteration in the silver of the moon could even be physically measured in a laboratory with highly sensitive instruments, but up until now no human has done it.

WW: What happens exactly when a spaceship is sent to the moon?

The Silver One: You change your past, didn't you know that?

WW: In which way is the past changed?

The Silver One: You are free beings and when you carry out such actions undisturbed then you change your past in a way I'm not capable of expressing. You're hopping around on the past of mankind, if I may put it so bluntly. This is a subject which doesn't cause me any joy. And when you send a probe to Venus, copper is changed. And you've absolutely no idea what you're doing to the moon and to yourselves when you leave space probes standing on the moon. You change everything.

WW: Please describe exactly what gets changed.

The Silver One: For example, the stages in the emergence of the mountains are retroactively changed. This means that the inner structure of the earth becomes different. Because of this, the teachers on the moon, the primal teachers of mankind are also changed. The wisdom of the moon gets changed. The problem is that at that moment when the change occurs the original past no longer exists. But not even we know what effect these processes of change will have in the future. It's because of your freedom that they're happening. And you alone have freedom.

WW: Are you afraid of these processes of change?

The Silver One: Yes. And if metal is afraid, so is the cosmos.

WW: Can you say what effect speech formation, or the ritual of the Christian Community have upon the etheric world?

The Silver One: Healing. Speech formation creates healthy words, and each single healthy word creates a healthy being. Every group which practices such activities creates larger healthy beings who move through the world healing and sacrificing themselves to repair those things which other humans have previously damaged. They neutralize the evil powers. The ritual of the Christian Community opens the heavens at the place where it's being held and allows the higher hierarchies to work directly through to the congregation and these forces then radiate out over the entire earth. The Christian Community contains much for the future, which even those celebrating it don't fully understand.

WW: Do you know your future?

The Silver One: Yes.

WW: Can you tell us something about it?

The Silver One: No.

WW: But you'll have a different task from the one up until now?

The Silver One: In any case once my human is dead.

WW: Thank you very much, Silver One.

The Silver One: You're welcome.

WW: To which group does the Silver One belong?

Verena Staël von Holstein: To the metal beings. They're cosmic nature-beings. They're beings found here on the earth, but whose origins lie in the cosmos. Some of the silver beings are also located on the moon. And friction can occur between them and the gnomes, for example.

WW: So the four groups of elemental beings were born on the earth?

VS: They originally come from preceding planetary incarnations of the earth, the fire beings forming the transition to the cosmic beings. Only the Stone One is the earth itself. He lives here and now. He's old and new because of this. That's why he has a different way of dealing with time. The Brown One experiences time roughly as a human experiences it. Elemental beings and cosmic elemental beings experience time completely differently. To describe this is extremely difficult though, because there aren't any words for it.

13. Little Glass Man

Wolfgang Weirauch: Hello.

Little Glass Man: Hello.

WW: What kind of a being are you?

Little Glass Man: Music. I'm music in another form.

WW: What tasks do you have?

Little Glass Man: I preserve whatever you entrust to me. Everything that is put into a glass I preserve. I keep it clean, pure and unchanged. I give nothing of myself to the contents. Actually I'm a liquid and constantly flowing.

WW: How are you connected to a glass?

Little Glass Man: I am the glass, and I'm connected to every glass. I don't like being connected to some glasses because they're not beautiful. I'd much rather be in beautiful glasses. There's also spiritual glass. That's used by the Nixes to transport their seaweed punch.

WW: Do you manufacture this spiritual glass?

Little Glass Man: You mean the right thing, but it's wrongly put. The Nixes need the spiritual glass, and we become it. We don't manufacture it. It's possible to be physical and spiritual glass. Spiritual glass is a kind of music.

WW: So music has a spiritual form?

Little Glass Man: Yes.

WW: What relationship do you have to sand?

Little Glass Man: It's my past and will be my future.

WW: Do you live in the glasses here in this place, or do you live in every glass all over the earth?

Little Glass Man: I'm here in so far as I can say "I". I'm the glass in this house. But I can spread myself out.

WW: Have you already been all over the world?

Little Glass Man: Yes. In Murano, in [Venice] Italy, there's some very beautiful old glass in an ancient glass factory.

WW: How old are you?

Little Glass Man: How old is glass? Glass was created through the melting processes of the earth. I'm ancient.

WW: What happens when a human blows glass?

Little Glass Man: He forms us and creates beauty out of glass. And in the process a personal glass being is formed for this glass. Glass is a totality. Glass is more than a material, more than a state of the earth. Glass is sand, glass is stone, glass is transparent stone and much more than you think.

WW: Do you also have a superior glass being and a hierarchy with different levels of glass beings?

Little Glass Man: Yes, and we also have a few unusual features. If a glass breaks, lots of little glass beings are created. And if the splinters of glass are crushed, sand beings are created. We're related to sand beings and the Stone One and we're the future, the past and the present of the earth.

WW: Is it painful for a glass being when a glass gets broken?

Little Glass Man: Yes. It's like being torn apart. It's a high-pitched pain. Glass being torn apart is a terribly high and sharp noise.

WW: Can you describe in more detail your relationship to music?

Little Glass Man: I am music. I am sound that's become form, sound that's become visible. Sometimes I make music and for that I release the sounds from out of me. For you humans that would sound roughly like a row of glasses being made to resonate with a finger. By producing sounds with glasses a human is showing what we can do. There are also sounds with which you can shatter glass.

WW: Do you hear the music humans make?

Little Glass Man: Yes.

WW: Also the music coming out of loudspeakers?

Little Glass Man: That's noise, not music.

WW: Do you know anything about your future?

Little Glass Man: Yes.

WW: Will you always remain a little glass man?

Little Glass Man: I can transform myself into sand, stone or light. But that'll only happen much later.

WW: Would you like to be human just for one short moment?
Little Glass Man: No. I don't want freedom.
WW: Not even for one short moment?
Little Glass Man: No, that's senseless for us.
WW: Thank you, Little Glass Man.
Little Glass Man: You're welcome.

14. Kahine, the Salt Child

Wolfgang Weirauch: And then we still have the Salt Child.

Verena Staël von Holstein: He's already quite querulous.

WW: Hello.

The Salt Child: Hello, my name is Kahine.

WW: Who gave you this name?

The Salt Child: That's the form in which you're able to speak my name. I developed it together with my humans.

WW: When were you born?

The Salt Child: This question is senseless.

WW: Why?

The Salt Child: Salt is structure and for as long as salt has existed, I've existed.

WW: What effect does crystalline salt have on humans?

The Salt Child: It gives the self or ego the possibility of forming itself.

WW: And what happens when a salt crystal dissolves in water?

The Salt Child: Salt always remains a crystal, in the process of dissolving the crystals just become constantly smaller. In the end the crystals become so small that you can't see them any more. Also inside you there are very many small salt crystals, especially in your blood. The ego which is connected to the blood, needs salt. Ego and salt are very closely linked.

WW: Are definite spiritual processes connected with the dissolving of salt in water and the crystallization of salt?

The Salt Child: A spiritual process is connected with everything, and a special spiritual process is connected with the crystallization of salt, because the structure becomes enlarged. Where salt grows in the ground the abilities for individualization of the humans living there grow. There where salt dissolves life can emerge.

WW: What effect does salt have on human consciousness?

The Salt Child: Structure-forming. It facilitates the processes of awareness, the processes of the forming of the self, the understanding, knowledge of the self in general, access to the human self. A body without salt wouldn't be able to carry a self or ego.

WW: Can one also take too much salt?

The Salt Child: Yes. Humans nowadays eat too much salt. What's more they eat polluted salt.

WW: What are you thinking of?

The Salt Child: Iodized salt. Humans are adding an impurity to the spiritual purity which is salt. And it's quite important to realize that when you eat polluted salt you're polluting your own self. It's different when you eat sea-salt. But convincing humans to artificially iodize salt is a great feat of the Ahrimanic beings.

WW: What happens to a human when he takes iodized salt?

The Salt Child: He changes his ability to know his own self. It becomes much more opaque. In its original state, iodine isn't a crystal. Through the iodine the self becomes surrounded by a sheath of iodine. Through the iodized salt it becomes harder to grasp the forces of your own self.

WW: So through iodine a human becomes dull in relation to his self?

The Salt Child: Yes. Dull is a good word.

WW: He doesn't really find himself? He doesn't, for example, find the task he had set himself before his birth?

The Salt Child: That's how it is. It would be even worse if iodized salt were used for christenings.

WW: Which salt should be taken?

The Salt Child: Rock salt. Quite normal saline salt.

VS: You have to look very carefully because iodized sea-salt already exists even in health food shops and wholefood shops. It has to be pure, non-iodized salt or normal sea-salt. Natural iodine which is in the sea, has originated in a different way and doesn't do any harm. The cheapest salts are mostly the best. What goes for iodine, naturally goes for fluoride as well.

The Salt Child: Fluoride is a halogen. Halogens make it simpler for beings to gain access to the human self and possess it.

WW: Which beings are involved?

The Salt Child: Many. There is positive possession through negative beings which leads to genius, and which is partly necessary. In the case of genius possession it is through higher Luciferic beings, who have missed their own processes of development and now make up for it in these humans. And then there are cases of possession from the regions of phantoms and demons which are sometimes only temporary. On the other hand, there are humans who are permanently possessed. It's a tremendous desire in the world of the Other Ones to permanently possess as many humans as possible. Because in this way they can achieve much more. It's enough to simply keep one part of humanity dull. They try through possession to spur those humans who are more active and awake to perform harmful deeds. And never forget that as human beings you're free and when you let yourself become possessed you must answer for it afterwards!

WW: Therefore iodized and fluoridized salt is inspired by the powers of evil.

The Salt Child: It's truly inspired.

WW: Are there other substances in food which have similar effects?

The Salt Child: Not in salt. Ask my friends, I'm salt.

WW: Thank you very much.

The Salt Child: You're welcome. Keep your salt pure!

15. Harmonious Elemental Beings

Wolfgang Weirauch: What significance does the angel of a Church community have?

The High One: The angel of a Church community feels he's a father figure for the community, putting it in human terms. Nowadays though he has to be called. Previously we came to humans by ourselves, nowadays we're waiting for humans to call. That's an important difference. The human being is the one who now directs everything.

WW: What effect do the thoughts of a Church community have on the earth and the spiritual world when these humans are in a religious ceremony?

The High One: They raise their souls together and in doing so enable space to be created for good beings, so that good beings from the heights of heaven can incarnate — though the term incarnate isn't quite correct.

WW: Incorporate?

The High One: No, there's no physical body, it's a spiritual body, a spiritual space. The term incorporate is only used when a physical human body is present. The spiritual space created is itself protected through the ceremony. Positive elemental beings can enter into this space. They can grow there and must grow there. They develop further every time similar conditions arise. That's one of the main tasks of religious ritual — the creation of spaces into which elemental beings and higher beings can enter. Beings always require space, and space created on earth always get filled with beings.

WW: I'd like to name these higher elemental beings, harmonious elemental beings. Are they created anew, or do they enter into the spaces created by the ceremony?

The High One: They enter anew, are changed a little, in a way they incarnate. Their own development is advanced in the process, and as a result they'll be able to take on responsibilities in the future development of the cosmos, which they wouldn't have been able to fulfill, if these spaces on earth had not been created for them.

WW: The human freely gives them new strength, new possibilities and a new quality?

The High One: A new quality is the best term, although words aren't suitable for describing these processes.

WW: What responsibilities will these beings be able to take on in the future?

The High One: They'll take on leadership responsibilities in the realms of the spirit. And they'll be taking on a qualitatively different form of leadership from ours. They'll also help people with spiritual tasks, teach them to carry out spiritual tasks which at present they're not yet able to see.

WW: So is it important for the people who participate in religious ritual not to think egotistically of themselves, but to direct their thoughts amongst other things, to summoning these harmonious elemental beings because in doing so one is serving the earth and the spiritual world?

The High One: It would be a positive thing if humans would do that. On the other hand it is disturbing when one amongst them is reflecting upon his finances. But it doesn't disturb when someone is dreaming or sleeping.

WW: What happens when people participate in the religious ritual who really don't like one another? Does that disturb the course of the rite?

The High One: Yes and no. There are karmic connections which lead to humans hating one another. But such a karmic connection doesn't disturb the ritual itself. It does however disturb the two humans and their experience of the ritual. Karma, on the one hand, is something very impersonal, and on the other hand very personal. But the course of the ritual isn't disturbed by it.

WW: Other than religious communities are there any other groups in which people sit together and such harmonious elemental beings are called in?

The High One: Yes, of course. In fact every positive thinking community which manages to overcome its egoisms and which is making the effort to strive spiritually. Such spaces are also created when friendships are formed with animals; smaller beings move into these spaces. The animal becomes slightly individualized through a human friendship with the animal, although its ego is still far away. The being moving into these spaces isn't big, but the process is a very important one in the world. All animals are involved, whether they be dogs, horses or canaries.

WW: What relationship do the harmonious elemental beings have to demons, or what effect do they have on them?

The High One: They hold them in check. The harmonious elemental beings are very much larger than you humans.

WW: Can you describe these beings in a little bit more detail?

The High One: I can, but I'm not going to.

WW: What tasks are these beings taking on at present?

The High One: They're in the process of finding their bearings. Their additional task will be to create better conditions for those coming after them. They also support communities. Unfortunately there are still extraordinarily few humans who are awake. Compared to the Grey Ones it's not sufficient in terms of numbers. In this area the harmonious elemental beings are active in a supportive, helping and healing manner.

WW: Since when have these harmonious elemental beings been in our sphere? For only a short while?

The High One: Yes and no. These connections have been a long time in preparation, and these beings are now more clearly emerging because humans are only now, at least in a rudimentary way, able to discover their self. And a group of people can create the appropriate spiritual spaces for them. The beings themselves have obviously existed for a long while beyond time. Though they've only been appearing in the human sphere since the development of the human consciousness soul and the end of the dark time. This wasn't possible during the dark time.

WW: What is the dark time?

The High One: The so-called Kali Yuga, which lasted roughly until the end of the nineteenth century.

WW: Thank you for the conversation.

The High One: You're welcome.

16. The Relationship between Humans and Nature Spirits

Wolfgang Weirauch: Miller, how can a human help the nature-beings?

Miller: By being fond of them. Apart from that he can help them by doing them favours, by trying to perceive them. But the most important thing for us are the positive feelings of humans, it's like food for us.

WW: Rudolf Steiner talks about how elemental beings slip into a person when he just stares at a tree, and live in him until his death and after his death are not redeemed but are charmed or banished back into the physical world. When on the contrary a human looks at a tree in all its beauty, the elemental beings slip into him in exactly the same way, but are redeemed from the material world after his death. Is that true?

Miller: Yes. That's one of the fundamental laws of nature and the spiritual world. If you want you can redeem the whole earth by looking at it affectionately and with awareness. If all humans were to carry out this process intensively and over a long period of time, the whole of matter would one day be gone.

WW: If all humans were to do it, would the earth then be spiritualized faster?

Miller: Much faster. Although it'll still take a while.

WW: Assuming one looks at a tree affectionately for a while, at that moment how many elemental beings slip into a person?

Miller: It depends on the tree and the person. That's very difficult to express in numbers. But it could be thousands.

WW: Then masses of these beings must be constantly streaming into people.

Miller: Yes, masses. They're quite small beings.

WW: So every day thousands of these small beings are slipping into people with every process they daily carry out?

Miller: Yes.

WW: The human being is consequently full of them.

Miller: Yes and no.

WW: Why no?

Miller: Because he's not aware of being full of these beings. After all, they're not in his physical body, but in his etheric body. And they're connected to him through something like a cord.

WW: Can you describe how an elemental being rejoices when a human looks with affection at a stone, a flower, a lake, a tree or at other spheres of nature?

Miller: Joy is universal. They rejoice in exactly the same way as you rejoice, and become inwardly warm and brighter.

WW: If a human wanted to help elemental beings, would a good method be to take an object in nature, to look at it consciously and affectionately, and at the same time to think about the joy of the elemental beings as well?

Miller: Yes. In this way a friendship develops. This works most easily with a tree. Every person somewhere has a tree. He doesn't have to find it during his lifetime, but he has one nevertheless. When a person chooses a tree it doesn't have to be *his* tree — a real friendship between human and tree being can then develop. They can then both really communicate with one another. Children can do it spontaneously. Children often know how a tree feels, to the point that genuine conversations can develop between them. Tree beings are relatively close to humans. The easiest way to get into contact with nature-beings is through them. Trees are very open towards humans, but first a friendship has to be established, like between my humans and me. That of course takes time.

WW: Which people have which trees?

Miller: There's no such thing as divisions into different groups. It's completely individual.

WW: How can somone find out which tree belongs to him?

Miller: Through feeling.

WW: Do you know which tree I have?

Miller: Yes. But it's not standing here. It's a cherry tree. It's growing on a meadow, close by a stream. In the springtime there are lots of flowering rape fields nearby.

WW: Are there any more things people can do for the elementals and nature-beings?

Miller: Yes. In former times the beautiful custom existed of giving a little from what one was drinking to the nature-beings by offering libations. You can also perform this outside in natural surroundings, by giving a drop of what you're just drinking — it doesn't matter what — to nature. It's enough simply to pour this drop out on to the ground. At home you can simply pour it down the sink. Though it's better to place it somewhere in the house.

What matters here is the gesture of sacrifice. The point is to give away something that you as a human are fond of. You shouldn't sit down and rack your brains about what for example, the house spirit likes the most. Give something that you like most and put it somewhere until it goes mouldy. A somewhat larger meal can be put out on definite days or as a thank you because something worked out very well. A good solution is to put this offering of food on top of a cupboard. There it can stay undisturbed.

WW: Are there other things we can do?

Miller: Being fond of nature spirits, playing music at home. We love it when humans play music. You can also sing us a song. It doesn't have to be a complicated aria like the "Queen of the Night," a simple children's song will do. It's also important to arrange artistic objects, to create a beautiful home. Spaces in nature should be just as beautifully designed. We eat your sympathies and we become round and happy through love.

WW: What do you do with the food that's put out for you? Do you suck it etherically dry?

Miller: Yes. We extract the forces of life of the food and as a rule it then becomes mouldy relatively fast. This mould is not a sign of a rejected offering. But please, don't raise any altars to us. That's not the right way. Altars are for gods, not for nature-beings.

WW: What questions exactly do nature-beings have for humans?

Miller: What is love? What is freedom? Why don't you see us? Why don't you assume your responsibilities? Why do you produce ugly things? Why do you use up the earth through the production of plastic? We do have many other questions but that would now be going beyond our scope. In addition we house spirits are especially interested in why you humans build ugly houses and why you pack your food in plastic containers. The animal beings are interested in why you go to bed together. The fire beings are interested in the peculiar heating systems and in why you pollute light and fire. And there are other questions depending on the type of elemental and nature-being.

WW: Nature spirits, then, don't know what love is?

Miller: Not like you. We know *about* love, but we don't know *what* it is. We can't feel it. Love is the essence of the human. The angels brought something else, and the archangels something else again. And that's why we're all interested, even the hierarchies, in what love is.

WW: Can elemental beings and nature-beings develop themselves?

Miller: Of course. We progress when we tackle new things. It was a tremendous step for us beings in this house to enter into conversation with humans. We had to learn lots so that we could start to have a dialogue. We nature-beings also had to learn a lot to enter into dialogue with one another.

WW: Thank you all for the conversation. How has this interview been for you?

Choir of spirit beings: You are welcome here. We'd be glad to talk with you again. We'd also like to put questions to humans. Let's work together, we'd like to help you!

[*End of the first visit*]

17. Madeleine, Lady of the Pines

Wolfgang Weirauch: I've brought with me a small round stone from a Danish island. Is there a stone being living in it?

Verena Staël von Holstein: Yes, a small stone being which was once much larger. Rounded stones especially have a lot of power. I also have stones like this, and sometime if I'm "down in the dumps," I take one of them in my hand and draw warmth out of it, even when the stone itself is cold. You can take such a stone with you as a power source.

WW: Are all the beings present again, and also today Oakbeena, the Lady of the Pines and Quadrom?

VS: Yes, they're all there and everyone says, "Hello."

WW: Hello.

VS: They're all very fidgety, except for the High One.

WW: I'd like to begin with the Lady of the Pines.

VS: She's especially fidgety and very nervous.

WW: Can you tell me what kind of a being you are? And what tasks do you have?

The Lady of the Pines: I am the protectress of the pine trees on the slope where the sun shines. That's an area close by where nothing more will be built because the ground is bad. I live there and look after all my pine trees. We look at what humans are doing with the woods and observe the odd ideas they have about woods with quite some scepticism.

I was very pleased to be allowed to participate in this project and speak with humans. I also have a name, I'm called Madeleine. The pine trees and I have a good existence because hardly any humans bother our area of land.

WW: Do you belong to one or to several pine trees?

The Lady of the Pines: To several.

WW: Do you have many deputies?

The Lady of the Pines: Yes, I've many deputies. But the really small

The sunny slope of the Lady of the Pines

beings don't like coming into direct contact with humans. I myself have a tree to which I belong. I'm not the woodland, but the head of the pine trees.

WW: When were you born?

The Lady of the Pines: That's difficult to express in human terms. I was created with the pine trees a long time ago. But as the single being Madeleine I'm as old as my present pine tree, and that's 32 years old. But the substance of my being is much older.

WW: Can you describe what kind of a being the wood is?

The Lady of the Pines: A normal wood is a mixture of different trees. That's how a wood being is created, which — putting it into your words — is a mixture of soil beings, tree beings and local spirits, and sits like a kind of bell over and around the wood. This being especially senses the paths of a wood, and especially the tracks of the animals and the paths of people.

WW: What happens when animals move through a wood? What happens, for example, when a deer moves through a wood, what happens when a blackbird sits on a tree-top? Does something change in the etheric sphere of the wood?

The Lady of the Pines: We don't experience it as a change, but as being. The deer belongs in the wood and has its home there. The birds have another substance around them. It's like a data channel drawn through the wood when they fly into it. They bring information from out of other spheres into the wood.

WW: And what happens to the wood when a person walks through it?

The Lady of the Pines: Then the wood's afraid.

WW: Why?

The Lady of the Pines: Because people with their modern machines cut tracks through the wood as happened recently here to us. This results in destruction and this destruction we associate with human beings. But it is different when somone takes time, sits down and for one moment is just himself.

WW: Can you sense different people? Do you notice a person who's walking through the wood looking around with interest, in contrast to one who plods through unaware?

The Lady of the Pines: Of course. The one tries to see us, even if he doesn't in any way consciously carry it out, and the other person excludes us from the outset. The latter strolls around as though in a crystal. When a materialist wanders through the wood, we experience it as though a crystal were moving through the wood, radiating coldness.

With the other person however something warm is created. We perceive humans particularly through the kind of warmth or coldness they radiate in contrast to animals, birds or plants.

WW: What's the difference between pine trees and other trees? Is there any communication between them?

The Lady of the Pines: We conifers have no serious problems in talking to one another, because we have the same rulers. It's more difficult to communicate with the deciduous trees. But when we want to communicate we use the wood being. Deciduous trees have different rulers. We don't harm one another but try to help one another. Problems always occur when trees are planted which are unknown to us. These are the trees humans bring from other regions.

WW: What problems arise with them?

The Lady of the Pines: Trees from foreign lands are very painful for us. Through them a process begins which causes us pain. But we overcome these difficulties because the earth helps us.

WW: I don't exactly understand why other trees are painful for you. Can't you speak with them?

The Lady of the Pines: They speak another language we don't understand.

WW: And how is it for the non-native trees amongst you?

The Lady of the Pines: Just the same. A further problem is that they take up other substances out of the soil. And that doesn't always go well together with our needs. That's why it can happen that some of us die. It can also happen that the non-native trees die. And death is a cold process.

WW: Thank you very much, Lady of the Pines.

The Lady of the Pines: You're welcome. That wasn't as bad as I expected!

18. Oakbeena

Wolfgang Weirauch: Hello, Oakbeena.

Oakbeena: Hello.

WW: What kind of a being are you?

Oakbeena: An oak.

WW: Just *one* oak?

Oakbeena: Each oak being has one oak tree.

WW: Where are you growing?

Oakbeena: Behind the house near the marsh. It's the largest oak, and stands closest to the house.

WW: What tasks do you have?

Oakbeena: I am oak. Oak beings protect. The function of oak trees for humans is to protect. Humans used to know that, but nowadays they've forgotten it. Here in rural areas oak trees were all planted as protection.

WW: What are they protecting against?

Oakbeena: They're protecting against the Other Ones.

WW: What happens when there are no more oak trees in a region?

Oakbeena: Then the Other Ones can get at humans more easily and can get around protective walls.

WW: In other words it's good when oak trees are planted at definite intervals?

Oakbeena: Yes, it's good when people plant oak trees around their houses. Oak copses are also very important in villages. You could also fatten your pigs in them.

WW: How densely planted does a network of oak trees have to be to guarantee protection from the Other Ones?

Oakbeena: That depends on the size of the oak trees. The larger an oak tree, the larger is the protected sphere that it covers. I myself cover an area with a radius of eighty metres.

WW: Are there other trees which protect in a similar way or is it only oak trees?

Oakbeena: Only oak trees protect in the sense I mentioned. Other trees have other tasks. Linden trees have another protective function and serve the sun being, while ash trees unite the Christ forces. Cherry trees produce the sweetness of life.

WW: Were you born as your oak tree grew out of an acorn or did you exist before?

Oakbeena: I did not not exist before.

WW: I don't understand that.

Oakbeena: You humans never understand. I was born as this specific oak tree grew. But though I was born with this tree, I also existed before. We always exist in eternity, even when at present we have the form we've currently assumed. You humans always have problems with this, although it's just the same for you. You're only Wolfgang because you were previously someone else.

WW: What affinities exist between people and trees?

Oakbeena: Every person has his tree. That is so because we trees are very similar to you. Trees are the plant form God imagined as he was still thinking of allowing human beings to be created from plants.

WW: Are there definite types of people who have an affinity to different trees?

Oakbeena: Yes. And all humans who have an affinity to oak trees have at the same time an affinity to Mars. If you're related to iron and Mars you're also related to the oak tree. Many trees belong to Venus, the birch tree and the pear tree, for example. There aren't so many trees which belong to Mars, but the oak tree is the most typical. Then there are many different sorts of oak tree, the common oak, copse oak, and various others, which we differentiate much more precisely than you humans. And every tree among these has its human.

WW: To which trees do most people nowadays belong?

Oakbeena: To the conifers.

WW: Why?

Oakbeena: Because humans need warming up. Conifers are simpler and not as complicated as deciduous trees.

WW: Why are the forests dying?

Oakbeena: Because you humans have started to change them. When, for example, you bring plants into the forests that aren't native to them, the forests need decades to assimilate these new plants. In the end new kinds of forest exist. But in the meantime they're quite sick.

Then there's an additional disturbance through people. When you humans disturb the planets which directly oversee us you disturb the forests as well. When you send probes to Mars you disturb the oak trees, you make the oak trees sick. But the worst affected are the moon trees because there's such a lot of debris from you humans lying around on the moon.

WW: Thank you very much.

Oakbeena: You're welcome. You could come and pay me a visit afterwards if you like.

19. Quadrom

Wolfgang Weirauch: Hello, Quadrom.

Quadrom: Hello.

WW: What kind of a being are you?

Quadrom: I'm the one directly under the house spirit, Miller. I'm so to speak the most senior deputy of the house spirit in this mill.

WW: Do you represent Miller when he isn't there?

Quadrom: Yes.

WW: What tasks do you have?

Quadrom: My tasks are connected to the sphere of moisture and warmth in this house. I regulate the moist warmth, that's to say, everything that's to do with warm water. You call it heating. These interrelationships have now become very complicated, previously there was just one stove here. In addition there were just pumps and a furnace that burned oil. That's all different now, and that's why we had to change one of us from the group of deputies, so that he could manage this new task with the heating. I emerged as this being only during the last seven years. I was previously more faceless.

WW: So you became more important through holding a new position?

Quadrom: We reconstructed me with the help of Miller, the fire beings and the water beings. Now I'm able to oversee the hot water system in this house.

WW: What relationship do you have with Miller?

Quadrom: A good one.

WW: Is he a good boss?

Quadrom: He's sometimes a bit crazy, but then he gets into trouble.

WW: Does it happen that you sometimes make mistakes? And if so, how does Miller react?

Quadrom: We can't make mistakes. That's not on.

WW: For a human that's very difficult to imagine.

Quadrom: You humans are very inadequate. You can forget, we can't.

WW: Can it happen that a task you have to manage is too difficult for you?

Quadrom: That sometimes happens. I then fetch help. Or something goes wrong. Sometimes you humans also set us tasks we can't manage. But then it's the task that's stupid, not us.

WW: What exactly do you do with water, steam and the heating?

Quadrom: I keep an eye on everything, and in such a way you humans can't even begin to imagine. For after all, you are inadequate. I surround the water continually, 24 hours a day, 365 days a year, and accompany its every movement through the heating system. That's a hard task, and I've quite a lot to do. It's a permanent effort of will.

WW: And if you didn't accompany this water continually, would then, for example, a pipe burst and everything go wrong?

Quadrom: Yes. The heating would break down.

WW: Thank you very much.

Quadrom: You're welcome. I'll stay here with you.

20. Knut, the Sandy One

Wolfgang Weirauch: Hello, Sandy One. Can you describe your tasks a little?

The Sandy One: Hello. I am sand. I'm the sand here in the region. Sand is neither stone nor earth. Sand is what for the most part the local terminal moraines are composed of. Sand is what the ice giants created as they came down from the North.

WW: What's the difference between sand and earth?

The Sandy One: Earth lives.

WW: Sand doesn't?

The Sandy One: No, not so, at least not organically. Just try planting a flower in pure sand. Then you'll see what happens to it. Nothing. It dies of thirst. We sandy ones just can't hold the water.

WW: But if water and sand are mixed together in a container plants do grow there.

The Sandy One: Yes and no. A hydroculture is created.

WW: Do deserts consist of sand?

The Sandy One: That depends on the deserts.

WW: It only has to rain once in the desert and then a whole load of things grow there.

The Sandy One: Then that desert doesn't just consist of sand. Then it's dried earth. I've never been in the desert and I'll have to just first ask and find out.

Verena Staël von Holstein: He's now asking.

The Sandy One: These deserts have to consist of earth. In these deserts the sun and the dryness have become so powerful that all the water has risen into the sky. If it were to rain there, something would grow. But there also are deserts of pure sand, and there are deserts where, in addition to sand, large amounts of salt are to be found. These salt deserts are special crystallization points. They're very important places on the earth.

WW: How exactly are these salt deserts important crystallization points?

The Sandy One: These are the places to which human egos descend who were formerly elsewhere.

WW: What does that mean?

The Sandy One: Human egos exist who were a long time on other planets. Sometimes they return to the earth in droves. The places at which they then penetrate the earth sphere are the salt deserts.

WW: How long have these humans not been in a physical body?

The Sandy One: I don't understand that!

WW: What kind of humans are they?

The Sandy One: They're humans who are preparing themselves for a new cycle of incarnation. They've completed certain tasks on other planets. For instance, they were a long time on Saturn and are returning now as a group to the earth.

WW: Are there many such groups nowadays?

The Sandy One: At present there are lots of such groups. That's why it's so crowded down here on the earth.

WW: Can you name such groups?

The Sandy One: You'll have to ask the High One.

WW: Does a sand being arise when a stone is crushed?

The Sandy One: Yes.

WW: One or many?

The Sandy One: That's a difficult question. Am I one or am I many? Am I a grain of sand or am I sand? I can also be a grain of sand if you want.

WW: You decide.

The Sandy One: I can't do that, you have to do it.

WW: Is there just one kind of being like you on the earth or are there many?

The Sandy One: Both. We divide ourselves up on a regional basis. And there are different qualities of sand according to the stone from which the sand originates. Only the really large sand being contains all grains of sand.

WW: Does crushing a stone mean pain for a stone being or even for the sand beings which are created?

The Sandy One: Joy for a sand being and pain for a stone being.

WW: Your creation was therefore a process of pure joy?

The Sandy One: Yes. We sand beings and stone beings are unequal brothers. Always when I'm there the other one has been there.

WW: In relation to *one* stone you're never simultaneously present? When a stone is crushed a sand being arises and the stone being must withdraw?

The Sandy One: Exactly.

WW: Where does the stone being withdraw to?

The Sandy One: Into the etheric cosmos of the earth.

WW: Do you feel sympathy for one another? Are you sorry that a stone being suffers when you come joyfully into existence?

The Sandy One: What's sympathy?

WW: Sympathy means for example, feeling the pain and the suffering of another being.

The Sandy One: That's a very difficult term for us. But because we've spoken to humans we've an approximate idea of what it is. We know that it hurts the stone beings, but it's necessary. We can't feel their pain.

WW: Thank you very much.

The Sandy One: You're welcome.

21. Moonlight, the Silver One

Wolfgang Weirauch: Hello.

The Silver One: Hello.

WW: What relationship does the human being have to the moon?

The Silver One: The moon controls your process of reproduction. No babies could be born without the cycle of the moon. That's why the children are also changed when you litter the moon with metal. Children take other substances with them on the way to incarnation.

WW: Can you please give an example of this?

The Silver One: One example are the children you call star children. This is actually a lovely term because the metals come from the stars. In the first seven years it's mainly the forces of the moon that work upon the children. But when the moon is full of iron, aluminium, titanium, wolfram, molybdenum, and so on, several of these metals penetrate into the physical body of new-born children. And this then leads to changes such as in the star children.

WW: Are these the so-called indigo children?

The Silver One: Indigo children is a stupid word, star children is much better.

WW: The fact that these children exhibit unusual qualities is because we've sent rockets to the moon?

The Silver One: When you send metals to the moon you change the moon.

WW: And that doesn't correspond to the being of the moon?

The Silver One: If you want it so, it will have to correspond to the being of the moon.

WW: Do these metals damage the moon?

The Silver One: They *change* it. Your sending metals up there can damage it if you want to damage it. It's above all a problem when humans act without awareness in relation to the interconnections already described. The human being is lord of the world.

WW: People do all these things without awareness. We send a rocket to the moon and don't know what spiritual effects it has. We know nothing about the spiritual being of the moon, we don't know the consequences for the moon, and we don't know the consequences for humans. I can't imagine this having any favourable effect either on the moon or on humans.

The Silver One: Everything has consequences.

WW: But they have to be either good or bad.

The Silver One: For humans everything has to be either good or bad. Though from a cosmic perspective this is in part otherwise. We change ourselves and you have to carry on living with it. If you don't wake up, you'll have a rough time, if I may put it so. But we don't judge it from the outset as bad. We're different from you humans.

WW: In other words you're saying that because people send metals up to the moon, we change the substance of the moon and also in the process, the substance of the newly incarnating human beings descending to the earth. Are there any other changes in children?

The Silver One: The eyes are for example, different. Some children can see as soon as they're born. They see the physical world straightaway. Normally, children can hardly recognize the physical world at first. A complete recognition of the physical world is only possible in the third year, when the self is more clearly present.

WW: Are there any further changes?

The Silver One: Children will receive changed organs, almost all organs, especially the liver, being so affected. This is connected to the blood becoming different. The breathing will also change. But it's mainly the blood that will change in its chemical composition. If you were for example, to investigate in detail the blood from star children, physical-chemical changes could be established. But you apparently don't seem to be in a position to make such fine investigations.

WW: Are these children sick?

The Silver One: What's sickness?

WW: Is their body no longer in harmony?

The Silver One: Yes, that's exactly how it is. They have much more of a problem creating harmony in themselves. Anyway all children have to learn to create harmony. And that's where star children have special problems.

WW: Does the growing number of allergies also have something to do with this?

The Silver One: Yes.

WW: Star children suffer from so-called Attention Deficit Hyperactivity Disorder (ADHD). How come they have such problems creating harmony in themselves?

The Silver One: That's because in addition they receive the strong influence of Mars. They're iron damaged.

WW: What does that mean?

The Silver One: I can hardly say anything about iron, you'd have to ask the oak about it.

WW: Oakbeena, can you say something about it?

Oakbeena: The molecular structure of iron, the ability of iron, to be magnetized has been changed through the probes to Mars. As a result these children have a different access to iron, they can use the iron in their blood differently. They don't just use it to transport oxygen but they can also transport other chemical elements.

WW: The education of these children is quite a problem because they can hardly concentrate and are hyperactive. Is there a medicine these children could be given to calm them down?

Oakbeena: They should have more to do with water, as much as possible with marshland water. Water corresponds to movement. Though they shouldn't drink marshland water, but bathe in it. Calcium combined with iron is also important. They should eat fossilized iron, in as high a potency as possible, from D30 upwards. These children can concentrate upon non-materialistic factors much better for example, they can follow movements and their spiritual tracks.

WW: Why is a strong Mars influence working especially on these children?

Oakbeena: Because they were on Mars.

WW: But between death and a new birth every human was on Mars. All incarnating souls climb down through the planetary spheres via Mars to the moon and then to the earth.

Oakbeena: Correct, but these souls stayed longer on Mars.

WW: And what's different with them?

Oakbeena: It's their approach to war and peace. They aren't more warlike, but more peaceful. Mars is now the planet of peace, and no longer the planet of war. The earth on the other hand is the planet of love, although in the human world that's barely noticeable. And the absence of peace on earth makes these children nervous!

WW: Moonlight, can you please describe what relationship the human being has to moonlight?

The Silver One: Unfortunately at most only a strangely romantic one. You like the orange-coloured moon the most, when it's looking like the sun. This orange-coloured moon corresponds to the human twilight zone when you love to hang your ego up in a tree in order to be able to wallow in feelings.

WW: And you like the moon most when it shines silver?

The Silver One: Yes, when it's silver, very clear and has a light halo. But you always then get afraid of the moon.

WW: Why?

The Silver One: Because the beings of the waning moon are then experienced most clearly, and present-day humans experience these beings as extremely disturbing. It's the same with the beings of the waxing moon. These beings bring disruptive forces to humans, unprocessed bulges in the etheric. Through the changes to the moon the beings of the waxing and the waning moon no longer correspond to the supersensible memory of humans!

WW: Are you also thinking here about the so-called etheric-corpses?

The Silver One: Yes, these are ego-less etheric elements, which are also partly possessed by other beings.

WW: We've already spoken about the eclipse of the moon. Can you please describe in more detail what happens during an eclipse of the moon to people and the earth?

The Silver One: The past is suspended, and in the process gets withdrawn from the ego. Because of this the Other Ones can get into the past and change it.

WW: What happened during the eclipse of the moon on January 9, 2001?

The Silver One: This eclipse was particularly impressive for my humans because they experienced it for the first time etherically. But on this day destructive forces also stole into the past of the earth.

WW: How can humans protect themselves during an eclipse of the moon?

The Silver One: They should stay inside, unless they want to experience the eclipse consciously. There's a difference. In such cases the eclipse can be experienced outside. You're then protected by the forces of Michael when you're consciously present and not seeking sensation.

WW: Earlier* you spoke about a thirteenth sign of the zodiac, the Snake Bearer. What's meant by this?

The Silver One: Seen from the moon this is something new which humans have to create. For more detail ask the High One.

WW: What did humans in the past do during the thirteen Holy Nights and the twelve Holy Days? Where does the essential difference with the present-day lie?

The Silver One: Humans in former times really experienced the thirteen Holy Nights as holy, and they knew there were *thirteen* nights, not twelve — that's wrong. The Holy Nights nowadays are simply not observed any more. In the past every farmer's wife and every labourer knew there were thirteen Holy Nights and acting on their feelings all behaved differently, for example, no clothes were washed during this period. Nowadays with the exception of the two days of Christmas and New Year you

* In the manuscript submitted to WW, see Introduction.

behave as though all the other days were completely normal days. Not perceiving the holiness of the Holy Days is the crucial difference with former times.

It would be a good thing if present-day people would re-experience the holiness of these nights and could perceive them connected to the respective sign of the zodiac, to the corresponding month, to the mood and to the hierarchies which go with them.

You can attempt this by keeping yourself as free as possible from day-to-day bustle during the thirteen Holy Nights and twelve Days. Of course, this is only partially possible because your life on earth goes on. But you can for example, try it for a part of the day. During these days you shouldn't undertake any business on the stock exchange, prepare for a wedding, begin anything for the future and not hang on to the past. You should simply be present and try to feel the day, the night and the corresponding beings. In this period heaven is open. All beings, the Mars beings, the moon beings and all the other planetary beings are present in this period.

WW: What happens when you do business in this period?

The Silver One: These business dealings aren't filled with light. They're ill-fated. At any rate they disturb the cosmic interrelationships.

WW: To which night does the Snake Bearer, the thirteenth sign of the zodiac belong?

The Silver One: New Year's Night.

WW: Did you intentionally arrange your book project so that on the twelve Holy Days always another being spoke?

The Silver One: Yes. And we also assigned the beings. That was very exciting for us.

WW: Thank you very much.

The Silver One: You're welcome.

22. The Paper Being

Wolfgang Weirauch: Paper Being, are you there again?

The Paper Being: I'm always there where there's paper.

WW: You bear the spiritual aspect of everything that's written and read everything humans write. Do you understand every language?

The Paper Being: Yes.

WW: Are there any languages you understand better than others?

The Paper Being: Yes. Languages that are no longer spoken, the so-called dead languages, I have difficulty understanding. And I don't like Esperanto at all. This language has no being.

WW: Which language do you like the most?

The Paper Being: Russian.

WW: Why?

The Paper Being: Because Russian has words which will be important in the future.

WW: Which language don't you like from among the spoken languages?

The Paper Being: Mandarin Chinese.

WW: Why not?

The Paper Being: It's unnaturally complicated.

WW: How about German?

The Paper Being: German is at present a necessity. At the present time German and English have the best terms for expressing contemporary life. So I have to be proficient in these languages. Though English is smoother than German.

WW: And how about French?

The Paper Being: French is irrelevant. The language exists but has no great significance in the present.

WW: How about Arabic?

The Paper Being: Arabic has to change and will change. Through the Persians, Arabic will experience a marked change and as a result will also have the possibility of grasping terms for the future.

WW: How about Latin?

The Paper Being: That's a terrible language, a dead language.

WW: Is classical Greek more living?

The Paper Being: Classical Greek is still embedded in the heads of humanists, but doesn't actually have any relevance any more. There are writings in Classical Greek which were very important at the time but nowadays good translations are considerably more appropriate.

WW: Does the physical paper mask the spiritual aspect of what's written on it?

The Paper Being: I don't understand that. I don't mask anything.

WW: When a human really thinks a thought, in other words, is living in the spiritual aspect of an idea, and then writes this thought down on a piece of paper, he's manifesting the thought in the physical world. Doesn't the living quality of this thought die on the paper?

The Paper Being: It exists not just on the paper but also at the same time in the Akashic chronicle. And if it's a qualitatively significant thought that has been vividly conceived then it'll also be written in some of the stars.

WW: How is it with emails; do you read these as well?

The Paper Being: Yes, but they have a completely different quality. Emails are fleeting. Emails are almost a kind of thought, but forced into matter.

WW: Are there any repercussions for you when a human writes a word incorrectly?

The Paper Being: That's his problem. The main point is the thought connected to the word. It makes no difference to me how the words are written.

WW: Do you also live in paintings?

The Paper Being: When it's art, I like being in pictures. But that has a completely different quality.

WW: Do you have a favourite painter?

The Paper Being: Yes, Michelangelo.

WW: Can you please describe in more detail what happens spiritually when books are burned?

The Paper Being: Something quite terrible. The very opposite to what is intended by those doing the burning. When books are burned with the intention of eradicating their intellectual content and not because one needs a warm room, then the content of these books is burned into the world chronicle in words of flame. And the contents are much more distinct in the world chronicle through these flames than if those books hadn't been burned. But you shouldn't intentionally do it in order to impress certain contents into the world chronicle. It isn't a good thing when something is written in words of flame.

WW: What were the effects of the Nazi book burnings?

The Paper Being: The same. The changes in the USSR under Gorbachev came about because the content of the burned books swung back from out of the cosmos.

WW: Do the Russians and the Germans have a special relationship?

The Paper Being: Yes, an exceptionally intense one.

WW: Based on what?

The Paper Being: The future lies in Russia.

WW: You said you can change something that's already been written. I don't understand that. How is that possible?

The Paper Being: I'm not allowed to make such a change without permission. About two thousand years ago we so changed many written records that you did not succeed in proving the existence of Christ by means of documents.

WW: Could you today also change something written?

The Paper Being: Normally not. But sometimes there are instructions from the upper hierarchies and then I can do it. Only then am I allowed to do it. I can't do it based on my own decision.

WW: How is something already written down changed?

The Paper Being: It changes itself. We shift ourselves, inwardly, and then something different is generated on the paper or on the material carrying the words such as parchment or papyrus.

WW: That's difficult to believe.

The Paper Being: It's quite easy.

WW: If I write something now on a piece of paper you'd then be capable of changing what I'd written?

The Paper Being: I'm not allowed to, but I could.

WW: Thank you very much.

The Paper Being: You're welcome.

23. Kahine, the Salt Child

Wolfgang Weirauch: Kahine, Can you please outline in more detail what happens during the crystallization process of salt?

The Salt Child: We coalesce and the image of the earth arises. Every salt crystal, even the smallest, is a cube. All of the six sides are the same size. And this cube is the spiritual image of the earth.

WW: To what extent is the earth salt?

The Salt Child: The earth is salt because it forms the human self. The place where the human self should become self-aware is represented by salt. Salt is the expression for the forming forces of the self.

WW: How many salt beings are there?

The Salt Child: Many.

WW: For which sphere are you responsible?

The Salt Child: Here in the ground there are many salt domes. The higher salt beings have decided that in my sphere of activity I'm to represent salt. I'm a salt child, not a higher salt being.

WW: Where are the higher salt beings to be found?

The Salt Child: The higher beings of the salt desert are different from the higher beings of the salt dome. Some are to be found on the earth, and others within it. In their original form the higher salt beings are those beings which are connected to the salt domes. Salt deserts are dried-up seas and the higher salt beings living there have been created differently.

WW: Are you just responsible for cooking salt or for other salts as well?

The Salt Child: Actually I'm cooking salt, but I'm closely related to other salts. We're close brothers.

WW: Are salt beings also connected to the salt one buys in the supermarket?

The Salt Child: Small salt beings, yes.

WW: What happens to you when salt is dissolved in water?

The Salt Child: I become more etheric, less tangible. But I remain present.

WW: Are you also responsible for sugar?

The Salt Child: No.

WW: Don't you like sugar?

The Salt Child: No.

WW: Why not?

The Salt Child: Sugar disagrees with me. Although it depends on the kind of sugar. There's sugar as crystallized sweetness and there's cold sugar. And this cold sugar is terrible, for it's created via a cold process and tainted with death.

I'm thinking here about beet sugar. Beet sugar is produced by cold processes in the soil. Beets grow in the ground. For them to become sweet they need cold. That's why sugar beet is best harvested after the first frost. The sugar content is then at its highest. This is the inverse of fruit formation.

All other sugars, from cane sugar to honey through to all fruit sugars, are produced by a warmth process, by the sun process. That's why humans who need love also have a voracious appetite for sweet things. They sense the love of the sun in the sugar. When they satisfy this need for love through a sugar that's been produced by a cold process, then the whole thing is turned upside down. That's why they want more and more sugar, and that's the start of sugar addiction.

WW: What should be done with someone who's addicted to sugar?

The Salt Child: What do you do with an addict? You try to stabilize his inner self and give it back its forming power. Every addiction is a problem of self.

WW: Thank you very much.

The Salt Child: You're welcome.

24. The Brown One

Wolfgang Weirauch: Is the Brown One there?

The Brown One: If it has to be.

WW: A ram has just died. Did you know it was going to die?

The Brown One: Yes.

WW: Why didn't you point it out to the humans?

The Brown One: Because it's nothing to do with them.

WW: Why did it have to die?

The Brown One: It was sick. That's why it was better for it to die.

WW: Could some day someone acquire the ability to grow fusions between humans and animals, so-called chimaera?

The Brown One: The ability?! It'll soon be attempted. It won't take all that long. Though from my point of view I wouldn't describe it as an ability. But some things will come out of the attempts.

WW: What?

The Brown One: They'll be bodies into which Ahrimanic beings will enter, who otherwise wouldn't be able to get a physical body.

WW: What kind of beings are they exactly?

The Brown One: In the foreseeable future there'll be a lot fewer humans on the earth. The development of the world population will go into reverse again, there won't be more humans, instead there'll be far fewer. And then there'll be many small Ahrimanic beings who otherwise slip into a physical body with the human, but who now won't have any human. These beings will then induce humans to cultivate bodies into which they can slip. These will be similar to human bodies.

WW: When will this be?

The Brown One: I can't give you an exact year. Numbers don't interest me.

WW: Why will there be fewer humans in the foreseeable future?

The Brown One: Because the culmination point has passed.

WW: Will humans die from catastrophes or wars or will the population decline through normal factors?

The Brown One: Both reasons. Many catastrophes will come in which many humans will die. In addition there'll be fewer and fewer humans wanting to incarnate.

WW: Thank you very much.

The Brown One: You're welcome. Be caring towards animals!

25. Gnunno, the Green One

Wolfgang Weirauch: Hello. Can you tell me how long you've been living in this area?

The Green One: A long time.

WW: What does that mean?

The Green One: How long have there been plants in this area?

WW: No idea. At any rate a very long time.

The Green One: And that's how long I've been living here.

WW: What did the world look like in former times before there were any humans?

The Green One: Quite different. The ice came and then retreated. The ice then came again, and then this ice also retreated. Afterwards the plants returned. In the past the air and the air spirits were completely different and that's why living things were all quite different in those days.

WW: What was different with the air in those days?

The Green One: Not only the air but also the light was different. You couldn't even have seen with your present-day eyes in those times. Humans imagine they can reproduce the past with their explanatory models. But the animals in those days were totally different to what humans today imagine, because the air was different. The dinosaurs of primeval times had different lungs. The air was thicker and more watery and the dinosaurs had to breathe differently. They also had a special skin because it was in contact with a somewhat different air from present-day air. This is hard to describe in human words. I'll send you an image — but you probably won't be able to perceive it.

WW: Like a fish.

The Green One: Yes, good. You can do it.

WW: Why did the dinosaurs die?

The Green One: Because the air changed. That was a slow process. It's similar to the Mystery of Golgotha, as you call it. There was also one incisive moment but nevertheless a slow process in which the groundwork was laid. Because the air changed the dinosaurs couldn't breathe anymore.

WW: Is it true that in the past the people in this region were mainly born in winter and especially at Christmas time?

The Green One: Why are you asking a plant being?

WW: Because you know the past.

The Green One: I know a lot about growth and decay. It was really necessary for the humans in those days to be born during the thirteen Holy Nights! And so they attempted to arrange it accordingly. The rhythms of the year were like that.

WW: And a boy who was born on the Holy Night later became king?

The Green One: Nowadays you say king, but he was the leader of a tribe. For us the spiritual equivalent is actually an initiate.

WW: Were no humans then born in the summer months?

The Green One: Of course there were exceptions. But they were regarded as a disgrace.

WW: Were the children killed?

The Green One: Sometimes they ended up in the marsh. When the marsh gave them back they were kept.

WW: When you compare the humans of the past with the humans of today, how do they differ from one another?

The Green One: The humans of the past weren't really spiritually present. They were more like a herd. That's why they needed their leaders. For they possessed a greater spiritual clarity.

WW: Which humans do you like best, the present-day ones or the ones from then?

The Green One: They are not there to please me.

Verena Staël von Holstein: The Green One is surprised by your question. For the beings who look after something, it's not a question of whether something pleases them. These are human terms for which they first have to gradually acquire a taste. They could certainly work together better with the humans of former times but these beings don't judge that.

26. Kapuvu, the Stone One

Wolfgang Weirauch: Kapuvu, are you there?

The Stone One: I've always been there. I already said hello.

WW: Can you tell me something about the significance of dreams during the thirteen Holy Nights?

The Stone One: When he will have seen the dreams then he had had seen what in the corresponding period of time will have happened.

WW: Which days represent which periods?

The Stone One: January — not your calendar January — corresponds to the first Holy Night, and then it carries on like that. It's actually quite easy.

WW: What happens when humans pump oil out of the earth for example in Saudi Arabia or in Iraq?

The Stone One: When humans have made holes in the ground, there shouldn't have been any holes in the ground. Always there where hollow places have been created beings of a different kind enter because space has had been made for them. When you humans will have so changed this piece of ground, you'll have had problems at this spot.

WW: What kind of problems are they?

The Stone One: Huge! They will have been huge.

WW: Can you give an example?

The Stone One: That's difficult in the German language, it can have been better put in Russian. These beings will have fought against the disappearance of matter because it will have threatened their existence. They will attempt to devour the spiritual impulse that will have had resulted in the dematerialization of the earth.

WW: The Ahrimanic beings feel their existence threatened by the dematerialization of the earth?

The Stone One: Yes, pumping oil out will have had produced huge holes, immense hollow spaces. That doesn't have to have been oil, that can also have been gold, cobalt or gas or any raw material extracted out of the earth.

WW: Can the raw materials be extracted and the holes filled in again so that the Ahrimanic spirits don't stream in?

The Stone One: You can try to have spoken with us stone beings. We can show places in the earth where such large hollow spaces can't arise. Many raw materials can be obtained by surface mining and then no hollow spaces arise.

WW: But that doesn't work with oil.

The Stone One: That's why it's a question as to whether extracting oil can have been good for the earth.

WW: Do the spiritual beings which enter into these hollow spaces have a particular effect on the humans living in these regions?

The Stone One: Most strongly on the humans in the region in which oil will have been. The cold destructive effect of these forces has been strongest above these hollow spaces.

WW: In what way do these beings work destructively on the humans living there?

The Stone One: They can induce the humans to slay other humans for rational reasons, with logical plans, to cause chaos, programmed chaos.

WW: But the humans who live there are in no way at all humans who prefer slaying other humans.

The Stone One: No, most haven't been so. But there will always have been some who will have been especially receptive for these forces. And these few humans are sought out by the forces working out of the hollow spaces. There will also have been many saints in these regions. If you really want to have known it so exactly — everywhere there are humans who are willing to kill. But many of them won't have done it. But in the regions where oil is taken out of the earth, more will have done it. You call it percental. Had you understood me?

WW: Yes. Thank you.

The Stone One: With Christ!

27. Eknaton, the Fiery One

Wolfgang Weirauch: And now to you, Eknaton. Hello.

The Fiery One: It's lovely and warm here, isn't it?

WW: Please describe in detail what you fire beings have to do with electricity.

The Fiery One: That's our sacrifice for humans.

WW: Can you describe this sacrifice in a bit more detail?

The Fiery One: I don't like doing it, but if you insist. When we more or less voluntarily give up the higher level of our being, electricity is generated. We go three levels deeper into matter when we become electricity. As fire beings we're three levels above matter.

WW: And you have to make this sacrifice because humans discovered electricity?

The Fiery One: Yes. That's right.

WW: Who determines which fire beings have to sacrifice themselves into electricity?

The Fiery One: The hierarchies.

WW: Are you the oldest of the beings here?

The Fiery One: Yes, I'm even older than the Stone One, but also younger. I'm also older than you before you were on the earth for the first time as a human. I am always new and always old. Fire was before you and will exist after you too. And the period in which we turn ourselves into electricity is not long.

WW: What's the situation with atomic energy?

The Fiery One: You should've asked Kapuvu, the Stone One about that. In atomic energy stone beings are sacrificing themselves, degenerate stone beings are living in it. This is an energy by which matter dissolves during its process of generation, but it's not a process of spiritualization. Through this energy, matter disintegrates.

WW: What do you mean by "degenerate beings"? Surely they are beings who've sacrificed themselves?

The Fiery One: What are beings who sacrifice themselves other than degenerate beings? They're degenerate because they're no longer themselves. It's the same for the fire beings who have to sacrifice themselves into electricity.

WW: The term "degenerate" implies on the one hand that a being has now a different nature, on the other hand it also describes something decadent.

The Fiery One: Decadent degeneracy is not meant. What's meant is that these beings who sacrifice themselves are changed through a process which for them is connected with agony.

WW: Just as all elemental beings had to sacrifice themselves into each denser medium during the condensing process of the earth?

The Fiery One: Yes. When the densification continues, atomic energy is generated from the stone beings. But atomic energy is the false death of matter.

WW: Are there also degenerate air beings and degenerate water beings?

The Fiery One: Yes. Magnetism consists of degenerate water beings, X-rays are degenerate air beings.

WW: How dangerous is electro-smog?

The Fiery One: Everything humans don't really control is dangerous for them. Humans haven't yet really understood the effects of radiation, also called electro-smog. They just imagine they do. Electro-smog is important for the progress of materialism, because it seals the earth up from cosmic influences. The cosmic influences are becoming stronger at present and the forces of evil are anxious to prevent this. Their intention is to increasingly shield the earth from this cosmic influence; it's highly probable therefore that electro-smog will increase sharply. Humans who want to look directly through the flame into the spiritual world should every now and again go into areas where electro-smog is minimal or exert such a strong will that they can break through it.

WW: Which is more dangerous for individual humans: a mobile phone, a cordless phone or a UMTS* transmitter?

The Fiery One: Cordless telephones are the most disagreeable.

WW: What do these emissions do to humans?

The Fiery One: They envelop them and repulse the cosmic forces. These emissions affect even the blood.

WW: What happens when there's a large fire, for example, when a forest burns?

The Fiery One: That's beautiful — not for the forest, of course.

WW: During a large fire do many fire beings work together?

The Fiery One: The angels tell us when a large fire is to be. We can't decide that for ourselves. But the higher fire beings are at the moment in negotiations with the angels with regard to fire receiving a little bit of freedom. The higher fire beings live in volcanoes. We'd like to have this little bit of freedom because humans are behaving so badly. But at the moment we're still not allowed to decide alone.

WW: Assuming you get this little bit of freedom with regard to fire, will then large fires be breaking out all over the place?

The Fiery One: Yes!

WW: Like the recent catastrophic floods?

The Fiery One: Yes!

WW: Do the water beings already have this little bit of freedom?

The Fiery One: Yes, because they're life.

WW: Do the air and earth spirits also have this little bit of freedom?

The Fiery One: Not yet. Only the water beings have this little bit of freedom.

WW: Will this little bit of freedom with regard to fire be coming soon?

The Fiery One: What's soon? Seen in the light of human years ... You won't experience it.

WW: So a volcanic eruption is still under the direction of the angels?

* Universal Mobile Telephone Service, third generation mobile system for videophones.

The Fiery One: Yes. And we fire spirits then have to work together with the earth spirits. The earth becomes new at the spot where a volcano erupts. Many of the upper hierarchies are involved in this process.

WW: What is the reason for a volcanic eruption? Are humans the cause?

The Fiery One: No. A volcanic eruption has to do with the life processes and movements of Mother earth. It may be that the hierarchies also sometimes see human reasons for an eruption, but we fire beings don't draw any connections to humans — not yet. Pompeii wasn't destroyed because the inhabitants behaved badly.

WW: Thank you very much.

The Fiery One: You're welcome. Always keep your flame pure!

Verena Staël von Holstein: Kahine, the salt child, would like to know if in the meantime you're eating decent salt.

WW: Yes, I am.

The Salt Child: Good

28. Valliniyu, the Airy One

Verena Staël von Holstein: At the moment I can't see Valliniyu. He's so light ... Now he's here.

Wolfgang Weirauch: Hello. Is the light during Advent and Christmas a special light?

The Airy One: Yes, it's different, especially at Christmas. Though it already begins in Advent. At Advent the angels "fly" close to the earth, and when the angels "fly" close to the earth, they bring with them the light of heaven.

WW: To what extent is the light at this time different from otherwise?

The Airy One: It's more dense. You could even measure it. But unfortunately there are hardly any humans who are interested in the quality of light. The greater density of light can be measured at Advent.

WW: Are you also responsible for smoke?

The Airy One: Smoke is dirty air, and unfortunately I'm also responsible for it.

WW: Does smoke mean anything else for you?

The Airy One: There's steam and there's smoke. With smoke solid elements float in the air, with steam, water. There are different kinds of smoke. There's the good smoke, incense — that's your name too* — and there's bad smoke, for example, car exhaust.

WW: When incense is burned in religious rituals, do spiritual beings merge with the smoke?

The Airy One: Yes. That's the angels. Shall I now describe an angel?

WW: No. Do other beings also merge with this smoke?

The Airy One: What's epecially important is that the words are spoken into the smoke. This makes the words visible. Whoever can see, sees the words in a different quality. And these visible

* *Weihrauch* is German for incense.

words are transubstantiated by the angels and the higher air-beings, and changed directly into their spiritual equivalent.

WW: What happens to the smoke in a black mass?

The Airy One: The same as with cigarette smoke — beings of death move in.

WW: What kind of beings are they?

The Airy One: They're the spirits of birth and death. But when they're called into the material world through a black mass they're chained to their death side. The most interesting thing about the spirits of birth and death is that they represent both sides. They either give birth or they bring death. And when they're forced to appear at the wrong place, their influence isn't good.

WW: What's the significance of an atomic power station for the air?

The Airy One: Atomic power stations don't produce any bad air, but they ionize the air, in such a way that inwardly the air has to vibrate. This makes the air nervous and nervous air isn't good.

WW: What are wind farms like for you?

The Airy One: We like them — they're like a toy.

WW: Thank you very much.

The Airy One: You're welcome.

29. Echevit, the Watery One

The Watery One: So you're here again?

Wolfgang Weirauch: Yes, hello. How does your being change when water freezes to ice?

The Watery One: As a Nix I don't freeze into ice. But the water becomes thick.

WW: And are the smaller water beings changed when water freezes to ice?

The Watery One: Yes, they become more material, they become crystalline. When the water beings turn to ice, they die in a certain sense and find themselves in a death-like Pralaya condition. And when they thaw out again they enter a new period of life. Many water beings regularly wander through the polar ice caps so that they can recuperate.

WW: Like humans between death and rebirth?

The Watery One: Yes.

WW: And what happens to the water beings when water vaporizes?

The Watery One: They become smaller. Then we link up with an air being and fly very high. That's beautiful.

WW: And when it rains you return or is it for you water beings a new life?

The Watery One: No, it's not a new life. New life is only created when we pass through the ice state.

WW: Who organizes when and which water beings pass through the ice state?

The Watery One: I arrange things for the water beings in this region. And consult with the other Nixes in the process.

WW: How do you experience fog?

The Watery One: Fog is good because then I can travel over the land. There are more water beings in the air than air beings when there's a fog and then we're so small that we can fly.

Incidentally we're quite round, similar to a drop of water. That's why gravity can't hold us so well. When we're in the air, we feel like we're in a trance.

WW: Are there also special fog spirits?

The Watery One: Yes! Putting it in modern terms — imagine a symbiosis between me and Valliniyu, the Airy One.

WW: Are they always created anew when a fog rises?

The Watery One: They're created anew with every fog.

WW: And do they die when the fog disperses?

The Watery One: No, they don't die, but return to being water or air beings.

WW: Over a period of one year, all of you together with Verena and Friedrich worked on your book project. Can you tell me how you've all changed through this book project and now through our interviews, because you've spoken with humans?

The Watery One: Very important. It has been more important than you could imagine, even you, Wolfgang. We spirit beings have to learn to understand your language. For example, doubt is unknown to us. So we've learned what doubt is. Then we've learned what feelings are. You humans should feel much more. We spirit beings don't feel in your sense. But we have to understand what feelings are, so that the earth can stay young for a little while longer.

If as our new masters we don't understand you we can't implement your ideas in the sphere of the elements. For that we have to learn a few things about you. Up until now we could ask the angels, soon — soon according to our conception of time — we'll only be able to ask humans what's to be done with the earth. And many connections we can only understand when we ask the right questions. That's why we have to learn to question humans correctly. And that's what we're now doing in these important conversations.

WW: Have you learned anything else from humans?

The Watery One: We've learned to communicate among ourselves and our mutual dialogue among ourselves replaces much that up until now we've received from the angels. In this area as well we've still got things to learn. You humans have one possibility we elemental beings just don't have — you can communicate with one another.

WW: But you also communicate with one another.

The Watery One: Yes, but only in our respective spheres, in other words water being with water being or air being to air being but between the individual spheres there's little communication. But now we've realized we can all communicate with one another. Water can speak with air, with fire and with animals.

WW: You haven't previously communicated with one another in this manner?

The Watery One: No, not in the way we're doing it now. Before contact was via the hierarchies, but now we speak directly with one another. Because we're speaking directly with one another, a completely different quality of being is created.

WW: So we humans have brought you to the round table?

The Watery One: Yes, and this has to be extended much further in the future. What we have here is just a beginning. As a matter of fact what we have to hear from you is how we're to form molecules. I'd like to know where and which water drops are to stay and when.

WW: How do the other remaining elemental and nature-beings who didn't take part in these conversations look upon you?

The Watery One: We'll become their teachers.

WW: Is anything similar happening elsewhere in the world?

The Watery One: Yes, but it's always adapted to the respective place and the prevailing conditions. And the conversations here are something special.

WW: Do you think differently about humans from before?

The Watery One: Yes.

WW: To what extent?

The Watery One: We understand you better. We see what's new about you — the consciousness soul and the first beginnings of an aware self. In reality you can do much more than you know. You'll have to fulfil your tasks and no God will help you in that.

WW: Thank you very much. We'll definitely be speaking again about one or other topic.

The Watery One: Gladly.

30. Catastrophic Flooding

The following questions were submitted in writing: What caused the flooding in late summer 2002 in the Czech Republic, Austria and Germany, and what are humans supposed to learn from it? What did the water spirits do during the flooding, in order to avoid harming humans or were they supposed to suffer harm?

The Watery One: I'll go directly to your question about the flooding. It may not be obvious but catastrophic flooding occurs particularly where the life forces of the earth are weakened. This weakening can be the consequence of a human system being in a place for at least seven years. Seven years is the minimum.

There are other reasons behind it, too. Let's stay with the human system. The forces of life are carried by water. Grand systems which hold life in contempt, lead to cycles of fertility, which are determined by water and the other nature-beings, having disharmonious changes forced upon them by humans.

The tasks of the Nixes and their rivers at present is to show humans that the way they work with water is lacking in insight into the wider connections, and that's why they're not capable of regulating the water. For the river beings these structures often have the character of a rash and playful experiment.

Putting things off is no longer possible for European civilization. If humans are not able to decide to collect up their technical toys, the decision lies with us to remove them and accept the resulting damage. As long as humans continue to work against water, water has a kind of freedom to defend itself. And when we become more "free," we'll also be able to give more freedom. Children have to be kept from danger. But there comes an age in which wanting to save someone from harm reduces their freedom, especially when the harm is a consequence resulting from their own behaviour.

Through the changes humans have carried out on river courses and, in the process, on the total water cycle of the earth, we water beings are partly no longer able to limit the damage. When we have to move too fast, we can't brake any more. It doesn't make any difference what's standing in the way. Much damage, not all, which we've caused is caused because you've forced us to it. Consequently it lies in your responsibility.

The water of the earth is the expression of the life forces of the earth. And as a water spirit I say to you, there's no end in sight to the floods, so long as you don't let the rivers flow their course!

The Stone One: There will have had been a time in which humans will have had understood what force they will have taken from the ground through their structural measures on river courses.

This starts with the treatment of the topsoil. Humans of the present have had persuaded themselves that with their agricultural machinery, chemical fertilizers, and their irrigation measures they have had positively influenced the fertility of the soil. The absolute opposite will have been the case. Where the gnomes, the really small ones, with the undines, the really small ones, have been constantly disturbed in their joint work, there will floods have been created. We can no longer have had kept life there where it actually has had belonged. We can no longer have given that which grows, sufficient life force.

Because of this, my little ones are willing to be formed into mud. Mud will slide! Have you had understood me?

The Airy One: It'll take a very long time for humans to understand that the water structures are decisively influencing even the earth's atmosphere, and thereby the work of the sylphs. This is again something different from the talked-to-death topic of "climate change," because it's not change, but compulsion. Humans are working on things the duration of which they in no way know, let alone comprehend. The air carries the water around the whole earth. And through the disruptive interference of humans, the water gets to places which aren't due to get it. The water is forced to act and in the process permanence is changed. A part of this permanence you humans call the future.

Strangely enough it's very difficult for a human to understand that time is a totality. Past, present and future are only aspects of time and permanence. And every change alters all three aspects of permanence, but not time itself as a moment. To throw a bit more light on it — permanence is related in a certain sense to one space, time is related to all individual points.

The Fiery One: Time arose with the light. It's the eternal concern of the light being to make this capable of being experienced. I'm simple. You can't yet understand anymore.

Can you imagine that the humans who planned these water structures did so with great commitment? And by doing so created warmth. Warmth is always created when you humans commit yourself to something. Warmth is also always direct spirit. That adequately explains my involvement.

Warmth produces fruit. Also the fruits of thinking. That's where it began. When thinking doesn't change, if doesn't become really warm, but remains cold and calculating, then the rivers also won't flow. Only love can bring change. Begin to love your earth again. Then you'll also stop doing such silly things to her. Then the water can truly flow freely. Keep the flames pure!

31. The High One

Wolfgang Weirauch: Hello.
The High One: Hello.
WW: What happens spiritually when two nations wage war against one another?
The High One: That varies. Even nation spirits can rub up against one another, but they don't fight one another. We good powers don't always have the same opinions, and there are often — putting it in human terms — problems of direction. The one would like processes to be carried out faster and the other slower. From this it's perfectly possible for wars to break out. In many cases wars are opportunities to bring groups of humans to a common karma, to a comprehensive karma. Because of this whole groups of humans can pass through a common process.
WW: Nowadays humans are informed through the media about everything that happens in the world. Is this in your interests?
The High One: Yes, we've taken a lot of trouble with it.
WW: What is the Festival of Michael?
The High One: The victory of humans over the dragon. This is pictured as the victory of Michael over the dragon.
WW: Rudolf Steiner spoke now and again about a Festival of Michael in the future, similar to the other festivals of Easter, St John and Christmas. What kind of a festival will it be?
The High One: The Festival of Light.
WW: Can you say some more about it?
The High One: Yes, gladly. How many books do you want to write about it? Michael is the Archangel of Light. In nature this reveals itself in the trees during Michaelmas time giving back the light of summer, by beginning to glow. Only at autumn time does the earth radiate light back into the cosmos through the golden colours of the leaves. This light can become starlight.

This process of giving back the light of summer is accomplished in two ways. One part of the light streams back into the cosmos, another part flows spiritually into the earth and cosmically reforms the structures of the earth. The light is weighed and judged. One part may return to the cosmos, another part flows into the earth and reforms the crystals of the earth. This is to be understood in a qualitative and not a quantative sense. This is the process of autumn: the measuring of the light. It's mankind's task in the future to shape this process into a festival. This is a transformation of the Resurrection.

WW: What can humans do to get a closer awareness of this process?

The High One: Be full of light! And now you'd like to know how you can become full of light? Fight the dark thoughts in you, and fight them every day, twenty-four hours a day. This applies to every human. When you drive the darkness away there's room in you for the light. If you want to convey this to children, bring them light, stories of light. Tell them stories which give you joy. And laugh a lot, for laughter is the vocal expression of the light. Don't live in caves in the earth, live in houses which are bright. That was a nice question for me.

WW: What changes to humans will arise in the future in relation to the perception of the etheric world? When will this form of perception begin in humans?

The High One: It's already begun. But many humans don't notice it, at most only a few. They notice it perhaps in that they're perceiving slightly differently, also in that their perceptions are more networked, for this is connected to it. Through networking they're looking out over their own garden fence. Networked perception goes beyond your own perimeters.

WW: Now you're thinking of a comprehensive perception, of every human being able to have an awareness of the whole of mankind?

The High One: Yes, this is the beginning. Incidentally this will also lead to more humans becoming asthmatic, because breathing will change when the etheric body loosens itself more distinctly. Humans will get asthma when they don't allow the new perception, when the perception of the etheric to a certain extent gets physically caught. The new perception will not appear equally everywhere, in the future it will be cultivated above all in Russia and Iran much more than in Central Europe. Many children today have it.

WW: What underlies migraine?

The High One: Being sealed off from cosmic influences underlies migraine. Humans who don't allow cosmic influences suffer from migraine. Something like this often appears at certain periods of someone's life, and when a human becomes more open spiritually the migraine attacks disappear again.

WW: Can you describe what the most urgent tasks for humans in the immediate future will be?

The High One: Act!

WW: There are lots of things one can do. Can you be a bit more specific?

The High One: Do what your heart tells you!

WW: That says something different to each human.

The High One: Humans have to begin to perceive the elemental beings and the spirit beings and act with them in the same direction. Otherwise the earth will disintegrate. It will die if humans don't take up their tasks and their responsibility for the etheric, soul and spiritual aspects of the cosmos. And then — this is very important — humans have to learn what beauty is. They have to learn not to just simply act and produce any kind of objects, but that everything has to be beautifully formed.

WW: What's most important for the personal development of humans in the immediate future?

The High One: Raise your children in beauty and they'll find their way in life.

WW: Thank you very much.

The High One: You're welcome.

32. Miscellaneous

Wolfgang Weirauch: I've got more questions on various subjects, but I won't address them to any one of you beings in particular. Please decide for yourselves, who is to answer me.

Verena Staël von Holstein: Miller will answer first, but not from his own knowledge but from the knowledge of all the nature-beings present here. They've just this moment discussed it and decided that Miller will answer you first.

WW: Which beings enter the human through food?

Miller: That depends what he eats. If he takes his nourishment from plants, a part of the plant spirits is still connected to it. If he eats grains, he takes in even more the forces of the positive thoughts of the gods connected to the grains. These are gods from the ancient Persian era, as the grains were brought into the world through an act similar to an act of religious worship. In the case of food from animals it's elements of the etheric forces of the respective animal which pass into the human.

WW: From the human point of view are there also any malicious beings which slip into the human via his food?

Miller: Yes, in fact quite a lot. These are spirits of the disintegrating, destructive forces. Because humans eat dead animals this food always contains a part which is destructive. But these forces are necessary, because after the death of an animal they provide for the breaking down of its physical body. You humans mostly assign these beings which are active in the forces of death to the dark side. But it shouldn't be forgotten that these beings are necessary.

With chemically polluted foodstuffs — and there are many of them — and foodstuffs with additives, other beings force their way into the human, and these really are negative. These are Ahrimanic beings.

WW: What do they do to a person?

Miller: They bring about a change in the human thought processes, because they change the brain.

The Green One: Chemically fertilized grain leads to the organs becoming weaker and the etheric organs no longer being able to reach their physical counterpart so effectively. Each organ requires specific cosmic and etheric forces, and when the physical organs are weakened these forces can only be insufficiently taken up. Each organ and every plant has a relationship to a planet. With an apple you're eating in the truest sense of the word Jupiter, and when an apple tree is chemically fertilized, the Jupiter force in the apple becomes weaker.

WW: Which beings force their way into the human via sense impressions?

The Green One: Here you have to clearly differentiate. On the one hand there are Luciferic beings, who bind themselves to sense impressions and can inflame and enthuse humans. When humans, especially young people, become highly excited or go into ecstasy through music concerts, then that's connected with the little red, hot devils, the Luciferic ones, which slip into the human with the appropriate sense perceptions. When perceiving with the eyes or perceiving something intellectually, dark beings slip into the human. They're called Fools and look like wet sacks.

WW: We've already spoken about these beings with the paper being. Are there also beings who bring about day and night?

The Fiery One: Yes. In the background are the spirits of time and they're working at each level down to the spirits of the hours.

WW: Which beings bring about the phases of the moon?

Kollii, The One from the Marsh: These are the beings of the waxing and waning moon. The effect of the beings of the waxing moon is to enable forces from the earth to rise up to the moon and with these forces the deceased souls. The beings of the waning moon on the other hand send moon forces down to the earth and these forces are experienced by humans as extremely unpleasant. The plants also have a different relationship to the earth during this phase of the moon.

WW: Are these elemental beings?

The High One: There's a grade of beings which are neither elemental beings nor angels. In the narrow sense of the word these aren't spiritual beings but astral beings. They exist above the elemental beings. But aren't yet really on the pure spiritual plane.

WW: Which beings bring about the seasons?

The High One: The seasons are caused by beings who are, speaking in pictorial terms, the lower end of the spirits of time. They're related to the spirits of birth and death. The cycle of the seasons of the earth corresponds to the life rhythm of a being. It's comparable to a breathing process. The earth pulsates between the northern and the southern hemispheres in the processes of birth and death which are expressed in the seasons.

WW: When should the festivals of the year be celebrated in the southern hemisphere? Is it Christmas there when we have Christmas, in other words when it's summer in the southern hemisphere, or does Christmas occur in the winter?

The High One: Christmas is a cosmic religious process. Christmas in the southern hemisphere has a different quality, but because Christmas occurred in the northern hemisphere on this day it's Christmas all over the world. In the southern hemisphere it's then summer.

WW: Does that apply similarly to all the festivals of the year?

The High One: With reservations, but seen from the aspect of a global religious ritual, yes. Even when the breathing processes of the earth in the southern hemisphere run in the reverse direction. The drawing into the earth and streaming out again of the cosmic forces in the southern hemisphere takes places in the opposite way to the breathing process in the northern hemisphere. When the cosmic forces have been drawn into the earth in the North, in other words in winter, in the South they've streamed out, and there it's summer. But the moments of the cosmic ritual are nevertheless the same everywhere in the world.

WW: Is my impression correct that through the climate change the seasons are increasingly disappearing?

The Airy One: The elemental beings cannot exactly judge in which direction the climate change will go. It depends on the actions of humans. *You* therefore have to know how the climate is going to be.

WW: What kind of beings are storm giants, frost giants and fog giants?

The Fiery One: They're accumulations of elemental forces. A fire giant, for example, is a leading fire spirit. I've already pointed out that fire beings in themselves are very small. But a fire giant is composed of many single beings, like "Ygramul, the many" in the book *The Never Ending Story,** that's a spider which consists of very many single beings. A frost giant is also very large, and that's why it's so difficult to warm-up a house again after it's cooled down.

WW: Which beings are involved in the birth of a human being?

The Watery One: The beings of birth and death. Seen from one side, it's the beings of birth, seen from the other side, the beings of death. From the point of view of the incarnating human it's the beings of birth, from the point of view of the dying person it's the beings of death.

WW: What kind of beings are they?

The Watery One: They aren't elemental beings but they belong to the somewhat higher level of astral beings just mentioned. They're beings which people should now start to perceive. People can't yet govern them but they should find a way of cooperating with them. Because the processes of birth especially are changing more and more. In a distant future children will be born in a different way, and so that this can proceed harmoniously humans have to cooperate with these beings. A particular problem in the near future will be that male and female fertility will decline, and women will have increasing difficulties giving birth. This will assume relatively catastrophic forms in the transition period.

WW: What kind?

* by Michael Ende

The Watery One: Caesarean sections, complications during pregnancy will occur more frequently. So-called accidental pregnancies will hardly be possible any more.

WW: How will humans in the distant future be born?

The Watery One: Through the forming power of words, through language as the precipitating moment.

WW: Is it true Ahrimanic elemental beings exist who are supposed to preserve the abstract knowledge of humankind for the future, but instead slip into humans possessing a disposition to psychic mediumship?

The Watery One: I can't say. But the modern media — media in the normal sense of the word, especially the whole field of computer technology — are incarnations of Ahrimanic beings in matter. All forms of digital recording, networks and so-called artificial intelligence are based on that. The processes connected to it are quite terrible.

WW: When a human dies his power of memory and the possibility of abstract thinking disappear. But all the memories of the human are marked in the Akashic Chronicle. When the human has died he experiences his life as a panorama, he sees his whole life because the power of memory has changed into a spiritual seeing. The pictures and thoughts he experiences in the process consist of a sea of elemental beings. Can you explain that a little?

VS: These elemental beings look like pebbles, I can see them. They lie around the place where the person has died. He must look at each single pebble stone once more. The Lesser Guardian of the Threshold is in charge of these memory building blocks. At the next incarnation these building blocks are reintegrated into the etheric body of the person if they haven't been redeemed or worked off. Otherwise they pass over into the universal Akashic Chronicle. The latter was just explained to me by Echevit, the Watery One.

WW: Is every thought that has been thought during someone's life also an elemental being?

The Watery One: Yes.

WW: Now we come to a difficult set of connections which Rudolf Steiner described in the following way: after his death the person realizes he is in debt to the world through every pleasure in life in his last life that he hasn't transformed into an ability. Because of this he has damaged and injured the world and certain spiritual beings. One realizes this after death. In the second half of the life between death and rebirth, two possibilities now exist. Either one carries on feasting on the pleasures through which one has run up a debt to the world or one resolves to settle and pay off one's debts in the next life on earth by transforming them into abilities. But in the process one affects certain elemental beings. Through the decision to develop abilities they feel injured, attacked and darkened, and have to slip into other humans. What do you say to that?

The High One: Guilt cannot be dissolved once and for all. Guilt arises through the misuse of freedom. Freedom however is the highest possession of the earth. The earth exists in order to make possible or to create the twin principles of freedom and love. When you injure another being, guilt is created, and this guilt cannot be carried by humans alone until it's been worked off. That's why as long as the material earth exists elemental beings have to sacrifice themselves in order to bear a share of the guilt. But these elemental beings can only do this when they give up a part of their light — and light is innocent. Because of this the human can act less burdened by guilt. When, though, the human doesn't work off his guilt in a new incarnation, it increases.

Particularly the compelling feeling of belonging to a grouping of humans — or to a group soul — causing someone to incur guilt can lead to cases of possession which in a certain way have something to do with the ability for self-sacrifice of the human who's possessed. This human takes something *upon himself*. This touches upon the Judas problem.

WW: When someone decides to pay off karmic debts through which elemental beings have to sacrifice themselves and slip into other humans, does it come to quarreling or to attacks, if he meets one of these possessed people in his next life?

The High One: Yes and no. The elemental beings are performing a task which is assisting the whole earth being in the cosmos. They're not angry with humans. But they're distraught when a human uses his liberation from guilt to incur heavier guilt. Then there can be attacks on these humans.

WW: What will be the greatest problems for humans in the future?

The Watery One: You really know how to ask questions! The greatest problem for humans will be the splitting of mankind. Two groups will increasingly evolve. On the one hand humans who can embrace the spirit and on the other hand humans who reject the spirit and will sink into materialism. Materialism will bring forth even more fantastic works of technical wonder, but the humans who have completely associated themselves with it, will not be capable of perceiving spiritual connections. And as a result they'll drive materialism even further forward. The task of the other group of humans will be to keep nature and the earth alive and not to allow the connection to the spirit to be broken off. At first there'll be many humans who will move back and forth between both groups. But the splitting of mankind will progress and intensify. As a result there will be many conflicts.

WW: How are crop circles created?

The Watery One: They're created by the wind spirits, they enjoy doing it. Anyway, we spirit beings enjoy taking the mickey out of you now and again. And crop circles are part of this, just like strange light phenomena and ball-lightning.

WW: Many humans claim UFOs and extraterrestrials exist. Is this true?

The Watery One: Extraterrestrials exist, but to my knowledge no beings exist which ride around the cosmos in any kind of technological device — apart from humans, who fly to the moon. We ourselves belong to the whole cosmos of the earth, but beings exist who have nothing to do with the earth cosmos. But these beings don't fly in space ships, flying saucers or such devices through the cosmos.

WW: But when humans claim they have seen something similar, what's going on here?

The Watery One: That's partly perceptions of the etheric but not of extraterrestrial beings, rather it's often parts of their own etheric body which are perceived. This has to do with the problematic nature of the *doppelgänger* and experiences of the sphinx. They're externalized parts of their own etheric body, and through the altered conceptions of nowadays they no longer look like a sphinx but like space ships. But these conceptions arise in the consciousness of the human.

WW: Rudolf Steiner speaks about one of the mightiest black magicians that has ever existed appearing in Mexico during the time of Christ. And he says that he was crucified just like Christ. Can someone give more detailed information about this?

VS: The High One would be gladly willing to say something about this, but needs a longer conversation and the time now is too short.

WW: What was Kaspar Hauser's task?

The Watery One: It was intended to make clear through the being of Kaspar Hauser that humans do not live from bread alone, that humans have undreamed-of powers at their disposal. Creating an awareness of this was the intention in the period of emerging materialism. Soon after his incarceration Kaspar Hauser developed astonishingly, revealing that he possessed special abilities. He was murdered because he was a claimant to a throne.

WW: How were the pyramids built?

The Watery One: The pharaohs and their priests were capable with the help of subworkers in human form in which almost no ego had consciously taken hold, of moving the stones with elemental powers. The stones were moved and piled up basically through mental efforts. This applies only to the older pyramids, for it changed in the later period. These were distant echoes of the forces the humans of Atlantis could employ.

WW: What was Stonehenge?

The Watery One: In the past, humans in the northern regions were open to the cosmos in a different way. Their heads were still open, in other words the spirit-soul elements extended out more than today, and this extension of the spirit-soul part is implied in the circle of raised stones at Stonehenge.

WW: Are there still secrets in the pyramids to be discovered?

The Watery One: Humans won't find anything more of significance there. For what's important about the pyramids is the connection between the spiritual and the physical planes. The base symbolizes the earth, the four triangles the forces of the spirit. The pyramids are the first edifices intended to make humans aware that the human body is a temple.

WW: And now a completely different question. It's about the so-called Family Constellation Therapy. In this therapy strangers are nominated to act as surrogates for relatives of a person, and in this role as surrogate they sometimes say things which are true but about which they couldn't actually know anything. What happens at such a Family Constellation?

The Watery One: At such a Family Constellation the perceptions of the person who is present and who desires counselling, are used and reflected. This person has a perception of his problem and he has unconscious elements of the problem in him which play a role during a Family Constellation and become partially unveiled. But the problem itself is not unveiled, only the perception of the problem and these unconscious elements.

The other people, the nominated surrogates, are so sensitized by this process, above all by the one who is facilitating this process, that they're able to reflect the problem. And they portray solely the perception of the person who desires counselling, and a few elements which until then he was unaware of. Nothing more. But it's made out as though the real problem was being unveiled. Remains of atavistic clan behaviour are used in the process, these remains are projected into the other humans. Family Constellation has nothing to do with intentional and spirit-based relationships.

WW: When we publish this book probably two different kinds of objection will come up. On the one hand many will object that one can't communicate with elemental beings in the way we're doing here, that this is only possible when one has attained a certain degree of occult training. How can one reply to these people?

The Watery One: Who's actually told you that Verena hasn't taken this path of training? She has already undergone the initial processes of this path between the ages of seven and fourteen years, by practicing pictorial clairvoyance. This is possible at this age when it's directed by an angel. This is of course no fully conscious training path because at that age her individuality has not fully taken hold. But she continued practicing intensively on this path especially in the last few years. At the beginning of our book project for example, she perceived me quite differently, namely as a kind of subjective comic figure, a being in pink wellies, but now she perceives me in a much more appropriate form on an imaginative level. This is also a path of training though not under the direction of a teacher, but of an angel. Unconventional, individually-based paths of training for humans will increase!

WW: Another objection could be the allusion to people who purport to speak with nature spirits and angels but who have egotistic motives or through whom certain evil forces impersonating nature spirits or angels are working. How can one tell the difference between you and these evil beings who disguise themselves?

The Watery One: All processes whose starting-point was a fear which has then been overcome because the moment triggering the fear has been transformed into something apparently lovely are to be treated with great caution. This is usually a sign of Luciferic powers. Luciferic beings are very beautiful, inspiring and seducing even to the point of adoration. That's why it's an important sign that one's dealing with Luciferic beings when humans begin to build altars to them. When humans feel the need to build altars to their spirit beings, they're on the wrong path. They can also be Ahrimanic beings who lead humans to believe something in order to make them dependent, and take away their freedom. They lead humans to believe they possess a profound intelligence and wisdom.

WW: Thank you very much.

The Watery One: You're welcome. It's delightful seeing you again.

[*End of the second visit*]

33. The Brown One

Wolfgang Weirauch: Hello, I have a few questions for you.

The Brown One: You can ask anything you want.

WW: Can you explain a little about yourself and your tasks?

The Brown One: My humans call me the Brown One, because I appear brown, but I don't give myself any name. If need be I call myself after the animal that I'm looking after at the time. My task is to care for the animals kept here by humans — pigs, cows, sheep and to a lesser extent cats and dogs. I don't need to worry so much about cats and dogs as they're very attached to humans and basically fall in love with them. I look after the poultry as well although here I have a faithful assistant, Vitchvydida, the Grey One, a female bird, who's so shy she doesn't want to say anything here. But when she's got problems she comes to me.

WW: What were your tasks before when there weren't any animals here on the farm?

The Brown One: There were animals on other farms. I'm not so bound to this farm as Miller.

WW: And did you exist before there were any domestic animals?

The Brown One: No, only after that was I created, so to speak. But that was a long time ago, shortly after the end of the last Ice Age. At that time the people in this region had their herds of Heidschnucken sheep, an ancient breed native to here. Since that time I've existed.

WW: What arises between an animal and a human when they become friends?

The Brown One: A new piece of friendship, that can form a space for other beings, that is, positive beings who belong to the ascending spirit. When a human makes friends with an animal, and the animal with him — as it takes two to make a friendship — spaces are created. And beings always fill up these spiritual spaces. You would include these among the harmonious elemental beings.

WW: How do you care for the various animals?

The Brown One: My chief task is to explain humans and their behaviour to the animals. The animals are often shocked by the behaviour of humans. Therefore I go to the animals — from time to time to the group animal, the animal "ego" — to explain human behaviour to them. When the animals are kept in a natural environment this task is easy. But in the case of animals kept in crowded conditions I have to do much more because I also have to help them just to survive. These animal souls are so miserable they need a being who's constantly comforting them. For you humans it would be roughly like someone having to live the whole of your life isolated in a prison cell, and then on top of that being constantly given disgusting food which you can't refuse. These animals are greatly in need of comfort. I sing children's songs to them — as you would put it in human words — so that these animals simply feel some warmth.

WW: What's the effect of straw on animals?

The Brown One: Straw is concentrated sunlight, concentrated ripeness mediated through the sun. Thousands of years ago grass was transformed into grain through initiates and higher spiritual beings, and since then grain has the ability to unite in itself the warmth and the light of the sun. And straw is constantly releasing these qualities. For this reason straw can be used in various ways to warm animals, to nurse them, to feed them, to build them up and to stabilize their bones. In the past humans, too, used straw. And if you were to sleep on straw you'd have fewer cases of back pain. The only reason a straw hat protects against sunlight is because it's sunlight itself. And a straw fire is short-lived not least because one is lighting a fire that's already burning. That's why a straw fire doesn't amount to much.

WW: Do animals in the northern regions need more straw because they receive less light throughout the year?

The Brown One: First and foremost they need different straw. In the northern regions the animals need much warmer straw, because they lack external warmth during the long wintertime.

WW: How was grass transformed into grain?

The Brown One: Through an act of worship, through a form of ritual. The breeding and modification was an act of worship. This rite was a process lasting many years. It was a prayer. It's hard for me, to put it into words, an act of worship is the best term.

WW: Where did this act of worship take place, and which humans carried it out?

The Brown One: It was in the region you now call Persia. The names of the humans aren't important. I don't consider names important.

WW: Can you say something about what happens to an animal when it gets genetically modified?

The Brown One: I can say a lot. What would you like to know?

WW: What's different about a genetically modified animal?

The Brown One: A cloned animal for example, has no soul. At least it doesn't have a soul like other animals, a soul which has been planted into the animals by the group animal. The human, in fact the human who cloned the animals, has to give them souls. A cloned animal shares the soul with the animal from which it's been cloned. In the process the human being makes himself guilty. But he is not advanced enough to be able to give an animal a soul. He also makes himself guilty when he doesn't know about these connections and uses such techniques. You know, humans are also responsible for deeds carried out in ignorance.

WW: What does it mean exactly that these animals have no soul? Surely it can't mean they have no soul at all, because even these animals experience pain.

The Brown One: Yes, it's already got the shared soul I spoke about.

The stone of the Brown One

It's much thinner, so to speak, because it has to do for several animals. And an animal like this can of course experience pain for it has elements of animal soul in it. By the way, little Luciferic and Ahrimanic beings are in addition active in every genetically modified animal as well.

WW: What happens to a human when he eats the meat from a genetically modified animal?

The Brown One: It's not healthy. The human has to eat this meat because he's produced it. That's the only possibility left to transform it. You don't understand me.

WW: Correct.

The Brown One: By consuming the meat of animals, the human transforms it into his own life energy. It's important in the case of genetically modified animals that their meat be eaten, so that humans eat up their own disgrace.

WW: Isn't it dangerous for humans to eat such meat because demons are connected to it?

The Brown One: It should be dangerous because humans produced this meat. Humans are responsible.

WW: What happens to people who torment animals, torture them or misuse them for experimental purposes?

The Brown One: After death their astral bodies will go through similar pains as the animals, so that they learn what they've done during their life. And that's good.

WW: That directly concerns those humans who've carried out these things on animals?

The Brown One: Yes. Recognize the animals as your little brothers and you won't do such things.

WW: But we all use consumer goods, cosmetic preparations or medicines which have been developed with animal experiments. Aren't we all equally responsible?

The Brown One: Everyone is a little bit guilty but personal responsibility is paramount. The relationship is similar to the one between adults and children. You can't blame the children when their parents give them something bad. Humans who use cosmetic preparations or medicines which have been developed on the basis of animal experiments, can be compared to children. But because in the meantime knowledge of such things has become available to all, even those people who use these preparations and medicines make themselves more guilty. These people will clearly have more to answer for.

WW: In a future age, in one of their next incarnations, will there be a karmic compensation between those people who tormented animals and the animals or the animal group ego.

The Brown One: The animals will change and these humans will have to take special care of animals in order to compensate for their guilt. They'll become "animal carers" — that's what you could call it — in order to pay off their debt. But it'll be a long time before things get that far. Humans won't want it, but they will have to provide this compensation. I haven't been told any more about this.

WW: Why are you so afraid of people?

The Brown One: Because you humans torment my wards. That's why I always look if those humans who want to speak to me are agreeable to me. I don't talk to tormentors of animals

WW: Thank you very much for your answers.

The Brown One: You're welcome. Protect the animals!

34. Gnunno, the Green One

Wolfgang Weirauch: I haven't asked you at all what kind of a being you are.

The Green One: I'm the boss of the Green Ones who are responsible for the garden, for the whole locality and a few places in the surroundings. We look after all the plants. We're the beings who care for the plants. We're the guardian spirits of the plants. We also mediate between the plants and the tree nymphs. But I'm not a tree nymph but a protective spirit for plant life.

WW: What is a tree nymph?

The Green One: The being of the tree.

WW: I thought that was a tree spirit, or are tree spirits and tree nymphs one and the same?

The Green One: Yes, Oakbeena is basically a tree nymph. And the tree is also kept alive through the activity of various elemental plant beings. Every tree has its tree spirit, and other cultures also call this tree spirit a nymph. It doesn't matter very much what name they have, it's the same being. Tree spirits for example were called nymphs in Greek culture.

WW: What do you do with the plant seeds in the spring?

The Green One: I do relatively little with the plant seeds. I protect them. The seeds are pushed upwards by the gnomes in spring. And afterwards the seeds are supported by the undines. I myself form a protective space around the seeds, and make the connection between the seeds and the higher plant. Nowadays you call it channelling. I channel the connection of the seed to the higher plant.

WW: What is the higher plant?

The Green One: It's relatively far away, and its level of awareness is similar to that of the sleeping state of the human. The all-embracing higher plant is as varied as the many kinds of plants that exist. But also each type of plant has a higher plant, in other words there is *one* daisy, *one* rose, and even each type of grass has a higher plant.

WW: When a plant is genetically modified what is then changed for the higher plant on the spiritual level?

The Green One: Life is changed. The plants represent the forces of life. When you humans change the life of plants you change the life of the whole world. A genetically engineered change is a violent change. Something gets cut. With every genetically modified plant you change the etheric body of the earth. Have you no idea at all what you're doing? Don't you know what will happen in the future through life being changed?

WW: No, people don't know. Can you say something about these coming changes?

The Green One: I'm not allowed to. Anyway, it's your freedom.

WW: Is something also changed in the human etheric body when someone eats genetically modified plants?

The Green One: Yes, because genetically modified plants have less life and because of this, the quality of the etheric body deteriorates.

WW: Do demons enter the person who eats genetically modified food?

The Green One: Basically, yes. Above all many more metabolic disorders will arise as a result. But you're making your bodies sick even without genetic engineering, because simply too little life is flowing into the human through present-day food. Every intensively grown potato or any other intensively grown food doesn't nourish very well, it contains very little life forces. The life force can't just be increased like that. Using chemical fertilizers doesn't increase the life force, just the physical components.

WW: Which plants have the most life force?

The Green One: That's a very, very difficult question. If I give you an answer now all the other plants will turn against me.

Plant life on the river — an expression of the Green One

WW: Then let's forget about it. What kind of beings are humans, for you?

The Green One: Do I have to answer this question? I'm afraid of humans. Humans are unpredictable, and that's why we dread them. But it's better if they talk with us. It helps us when we experience their motives. So much is unclear, they know so little of what they really want and that makes us so nervous.

WW: Thank you very much.

The Green One: You're welcome. Treat the plants with dignity!

35. Etchevit, The Watery One

The Watery One had asked me about the difference between the human ego and the ego of an angel. At this point I gave a short lecture on the subject of this difference. Etchevit had a second question about the inside and the outside of the cosmos, which I didn't exactly understand. At this point he explains it once again for the readers because I wasn't able to give him an answer.

The Watery One: Through Verena we have been able to look upon the one who comes from outside. We call him the Alien, the Antichrist. He comes from regions beyond our cosmos and my question is how does he see from the outside what we see from the inside. What's the difference between these two ways of seeing?

Wofgang Weirauch: Does Ahriman also come from outside?

The Watery One: No, Ahriman comes from inside. But the Alien, the Antichrist comes from outside. Many beings have already been called the Antichrist, but the actual Antichrist is this opponent of Christ, he's a kind of brother of Christ. He's the inverted brother of Christ. He comes from beyond this cosmos whose centre is the being of Christ. In this cosmos, in fact on the Earth, Christ went through death and created freedom as a result. The possibility has been given of creating a new cosmos. But at that moment, as a kind of counterbalance, a being from outside had to look upon this act of Christ, otherwise it wouldn't have been possible. What did this Alien see? That's what we water spirits want to know. Do you understand our problem? We could do a lot if we knew more here.

WW: Shall I question the High One more in-depth, or is it pointless?

The Watery One: The angels are all inside and don't know. Only humans can look out of the cosmos.

WW: Just so I can get things clearer — is it exactly like the Fools, the beings of stupidity, who are necessary in order that clever ideas can be thought, or like the beings of ugliness who are necessary in order for a beautiful work of art to arise? Does a counterweight always have to be present when something is meant to come into being? Is the Alien, the Antichrist to be understood in this way as a counterpart to the free act of Christ, to the Mystery of Golgotha?

The Watery One: That's right. I've just spoken with the High One. You asked him the question who was the black magician who was crucified in Mexico. He was the antithesis to Jesus. The Earth would have been torn apart if he hadn't appeared on Earth. The Earth would have physically broken up, when this antithesis hadn't existed in America as Jesus was living in Palestine. That's exactly the same principle.

WW: That was the most powerful black magician there has ever been ...

The Watery One: ... and will ever be.

WW: Rudolf Steiner describes that he was crucified at the same time as Jesus Christ (see page 194), and in fact head down, and that he was defeated by a human connected to an archangel.

The Watery One: That's exactly it. The black magician is the antithesis to Jesus, the human, and connected to him was the Alien, the Antichrist, who's the antithesis to Christ.

WW: Unfortunately Steiner only spoke once about this and I've never been able to read anything else in any other passage concerning these circumstances.

The Watery One: Ask us.

36. The High One

Wolfgang Weirauch: To what extent is the weather, especially the ever increasing number of natural catastrophes, connected to human unspirituality?

The High One: Human unspirituality is a problematic wording. The weather is an expression of thought processes on all levels, all human thought processes, unspiritual as well as spiritual. You shouldn't muddle that up. What expresses itself in the weather is what humans experience in their inner processes, both the calm and the chaotic ones. Well-balanced and controlled human thinking has a compensating influence on the weather. The more individual human thoughts become, the more transitory and more localized the weather becomes. And the more chaotic human thoughts become, the more chaotic the weather conditions become.

WW: What impulses come from the gods into the earth's atmosphere with a thunderstorm?

The High One: In this region it's Thor who initiates thunderstorms. When he fights against the loss of rhythm in the world, lightning is generated. And when he fights against the ancient beings, the giants, then it thunders. The idea that thunder expresses divine anger isn't wrong. It's anger against mounting egoism. And egoism is to be found in many places.

WW: Will weather conditions become even more catastrophic in the future?

The High One: Considerably more catastrophic. This is connected to human souls receiving less guidance and the ability of the human soul to form itself not being sufficiently advanced.

WW: What happens cosmically and terrestrially through meteorites?

The High One: That depends on the type of meteorite. There are stony meteorites and iron meteorites. The iron meteorites are very, very important, they're spiritual swords which come down to earth in the form of visible metals. All the important swords in human evolution — even the so-called double-edged sword — have been forged from meteoric iron. They embody in the physical plane what ideals are in the spiritual plane. The stony meteorites on the contrary have the task of bringing humans to their senses. Meteors are special spiritual beings. They move with the meteor streams around the sun, and during this orbit they load up with impulses from the beings who live "behind" the sun.

WW: With negative impulses?

The High One: Not only negative, also good ones.

WW: Can you explain these impulses in a little more detail?

The High One: By and large these are impulses so that humans don't forget the future. The impulses which arise from behind the sun will be realized in the future. They also serve to push back faulty spiritual developments which have arisen on the earth. For humans these can be in part very painful processes.

WW: Can you please give a few examples?

The High One: This comes about, for example, when a group of humans establish a community with a meaningful task and a positive goal, but take things to extremes and stubbornly go their own way without looking to either left or right. One example is the Salvation Army. It has good intentions but carries them out quite rigidly and fixedly. For such things there are many examples, and the spiritual world in a certain sense deploys meteorites against such hardening tendencies. Of course this is not to be understood as though meteorites fall down on the heads of some particular humans. They act as a form of spiritual cleansing.

WW: Can you say a little bit about the impulses which lie at the roots of racism?

The High One: These are very old impulses. In the ancient past there were reasons to allow certain types of human body to arise under certain circumstances. They had to have certain characteristics on the terrestrial plane. And in order to achieve this goal different races came into being. That was correct and necessary. But this time is long gone. Because humans are driven by the forces of evil, they still tend to emphasize racial elements and on the basis of external appearance imagine themselves as being superior to other humans. The races have long been in the process of dissolving, and it's the task of humans to completely dissolve these erroneous and destructive ideas as well. Races have no longer any significance.

WW: How does one practise understanding between peoples today?

The High One: Through language. You have to find a language all humans understand and which can express the content of the spiritual world. But it shouldn't be an artificial language. When language leads into the visible world then it represents in visible terms. Create spaces for languages. And create meetings at which people can speak directly from one human being to another. When people meet it's quite unimportant in which language they speak to one another, whether it's Persian, Russian, German or English.

WW: We've already spoken about human beings dividing into two groups in the future depending on whether they open themselves to the spiritual world or not. What happens to the respective guardian angels of these two groups of people? Will the guardian angels also divide themselves into corresponding groups? Do the guardian angels have to follow people into an involvement in materialism?

The High One: They have to. Guardian angels have to follow humans who freely decide to belong to one group. The guardian angels have no choice. Many of them will have to put on garments of black.

WW: Isn't that a terrible thing for the guardian angels?

The High One: What's terrible?

WW: When people, and as a result their guardian angels, don't take the path of spiritual development.

The High One: Human beings have the possibility of choosing. We spiritual beings don't have this choice and for that reason experience the horror quite differently. We continue on the path freely chosen by humans and suffer identical consequences.

WW: Will these two groups of angels also have to fight one another?

The High One: No, not in the spiritual world. The struggle takes place on the earth. The dragon is also at work on earth. It's now living on earth and I've played a part in this.

WW: Will this split also reach into the sphere of the archangels?

The High One: I'm not going to answer that.

WW: What does Whitsun mean spiritually for the cosmos and for humans?

The High One: Whitsun has still to come. Whitsun is what you touched upon with your question about understanding between peoples. Whitsun is the festival of spiritual understanding. When the Whitsun event has fully come down to earth, all humans who try to understand it, will be able to communicate with one another without earthly language. This will be a process on the level of inspiration. They'll converse with one another in inspirational ideas.

WW: What kind of a being is the Holy Spirit?

The High One: In your language the Holy Spirit is best referred to as the Healing Spirit. The Holy Spirit is something before which we can only bow — if you can understand this image. As God the Father is the absolute beginning of all being, so is the Healing Spirit the future, the fulfillment of all being. Do you understand me?

WW: Yes.

The High One: Would you like more images?

WW: Yes.

The High One: The Healing Spirit is that which as fruit sheathes the past, present and future. This sheath is like a kind of luminous egg. Christ can only reveal the heavenly Jerusalem when this sheath is fully created. In terms of the Apocalypse it is the bride.

WW: Can you say some thing about the tasks of Michael?

The High One: Michael is the face of Christ. It's his task to show humans — to be more precise, those humans who wish to follow him — how they can distinguish between good and evil and how they can let their freedom be turned into swords of light. Please excuse the harsh images but they express it the best. Learn to think! Learn to think independently and freely, and you will follow Michael!

WW: Can you say something about the human *doppelgänger*?

The High One: Which one?

WW: First the astral *doppelgänger.*

The High One: He's brave. As we've established more than once the duality of darkness and light is needed to make existence possible. The astral *doppelgänger* is animated by the forces of evil. Only for this reason can the *doppelgänger* be transformed through the human, and only through the transformation of the *doppelgänger* is the human capable of defeating death.

WW: Is the etheric *doppelgänger* the Ahrimanic being which slips into every human at his birth?

The High One: Yes and no. The etheric *doppelgänger* is the one who's instrumental in the outbreak and development of illness. He's not the illness, but brings it to manifestation. On the basis of his much higher wisdom, he's able to see the illnesses which are necessary. And with an infinitely strong will brings them into manifestation. In this respect he's a white being of darkness.

WW: What kind of a human was Napoleon?

The High One: A small one.

WW: I mean spiritually.

The High One: A small one.

WW: Did he have a human ego?

The High One: He wasn't always in control of himself. He allowed himself to be used by dark impulses. His initial motive arose out of his awareness of the equality of all humans. Because he went to extremes in this area he could be possessed. Though he performed many deeds in a dark state of possession, they also brought order. Europe became much more organized through him, which as a consequence gave Ahriman a stronger position, because Ahriman organizes. But that's also necessary.

WW: What took place in the so-called School of Michael from the fifteenth to the eighteenth centuries in the spiritual world?

The High One: You took part. Remember and you'll know.

WW: But I can't remember. This is a present-day problem for people that they can't remember their stay in the spiritual world.

The High One: Your problem is that you think you can't remember. If you didn't always assume you couldn't do it, it would be a lot easier for you to remember. The best human picture for this School of Michael is a conference. The beings are sitting in a circle and listening to the teaching being given to them. These teachings were repeated regularly because during the period of the School of Michael a few beings, mainly humans, were always incarnated on the earth.

WW: How many humans took part in this School of Michael?

The High One: Roughly one seventh of all human souls. But not every human soul understood the contents of the School of Michael. And on earth there's far fewer who can implement these contents.

WW: What subjects were taught to the humans in the School of Michael?

The High One: In the meantime they're available for the most part to you in book form on the earth. To these subjects belong the fourfold being of the human, in other words that the human doesn't just have a physical body, but also an etheric body, an astral body and an ego. This fourfold being was taught to humans as spiritual law and consequently as a path of development as well. On earth the fact of the fourfold nature of humans was — and still is — strongly fought against, the decisive point being the denial of the spirit or the self, though even the existence of the soul is strongly disputed.

A second main aspect taught during the School of Michael were the facts of reincarnation and karma. This is a question above all of human freedom, and about the other side of freedom, namely love. Love is the other side of freedom. Only in freedom can humans love. Only the free human can love. This has to get even further into human minds.

WW: What happened in AD 666 in Gondishapur?

The High One: In Gondishapur a kind of pouring out of future knowledge was prepared, through the forces of evil. The knowledge which at that time penetrated into humans through the Academy of Gondishapur was way beyond the intellectual capabilities of the humans living then. This would have led to a premature ageing of the Earth. And through its strict forms Islam acted as a balance to this. But this strict form has in many ways become rigid, and that's its problem today.

WW: Was the initiate from Gondishapur, who was the main influence for the premature wisdom, a Christian scholar?

The High One: That's a correct description.

WW: What kind of a person was he?

The High One: Spiritually he was a very great human being. He was very wise otherwise he wouldn't have endured these Ahrimanic forces. He underwent several stages of initiation. He was able to perceive beings who weren't living in bodies. He could speak with moon beings. And he was able to tap into the knowledge of certain moon beings, the so-called archetypal teachers of mankind.

WW: Was he a physician in outer life?

The High One: That's not important.

WW: As you've just mentioned the archetypal teachers of mankind, what kind of moon beings are they? Are they angels?

The High One: They're not yet completely angels. They were humans who were so far advanced they didn't have to incarnate anymore.

WW: Rudolf Steiner spoke about the faculty of mechanical occultism, which would be especially developed by people in America. What is meant is the ability to apply certain rhythms in technology and that humans can have a direct effect on machines. Can you say a little bit about this?

The High One: Yes. What would you like to know exactly?

WW: I don't completely understand how the link between human and machine will work. Which human forces would influence a machine?

The High One: Machines are beings. Indeed in the future they'll become even more clearly being-like, to use Kapuvu's words. The faculty of mechanical occultism is necessary in order to teach the machine beings. [*At this moment the light went out for a short time*]. Humans will learn to perform something along the lines of what you've just experienced with the lamp. You can influence machines through spiritual actions. That's mechanical occultism.

You can imagine it in the following way: from the human being who has acquired the faculty of mechanical occultism, something like a thin beam will stream out, penetrating the machine and activating its circuitry or whatever. This is a faculty to produce a kind of energy and to direct it into the machine. It's like a small bolt of lightning.

WW: Is it the etheric body or more the astral body of the human which emits this beam?

The High One: Neither the one nor the other. It's the spiritual being of the human. However, the beam is channelled through the etheric body; only this is "thick" enough to direct this energy.

WW: Is there an individual relationship between human and machine?

The High One: Yes, a kind of friendship arises between the two of them.

WW: Will we be using new forms of energy in the future?

The High One: Humankind will have to learn to use other forms of energy. The sacrifices in the sphere of electricity will have to decline.

WW: Can you describe these new forms of energy a little?

The High One: Reluctantly. A similar use of forms of energy as at the time of Atlantis will come but on a higher level. During the time of Atlantis it was the forces of life, of plant growth. Now try and transpose these forces on to a higher, spiritual level. Then you have the new energy forms.

WW: Steiner speaks about all the present intellectual, shadow-like, and pure materialistic ideas experiencing a sudden transformation in the eighth millenium and being transformed into a kind of network of spiders. These will be automaton-like spiders, existing on a level between the mineral kingdom and the plant kingdom, but vastly intelligent. These spiders will be dreadfully evil, they'll span the whole earth with their webs and those humans who haven't created for themselves the possibility of raising themselves to the spirit will become entangled in these spider's webs.* Can you describe these spider beings in a little more detail?

The High One: You experience their forerunner daily. You love it in a certain way because it networks you with many people. It's the internet. Now imagine the internet on a bioactive level and you'll get much closer to an idea of these spiders and their webs. It'll still take some time though, until the forms of energy we previously spoke about, become reality. But information processing will also be based on these energy foms. And this will lead to the creation of a kind of collective awareness of all humans.

WW: Will people then be so intellectually and spiritually linked together as they are today through the internet?

The High One: Yes. And some will become entangled in it and others will use this awareness.

WW: Some will succumb to the spiders, the others, who have opened themselves to the spirit, will be able to raise themselves out of this tangle of the spiders?

The High One: That's approximately it. That's a good image.

WW: In this context Steiner also spoke about so-called Vulcan beings, who since the end of the nineteenth century have been wanting to descend to the earth. They brought the connections of spiritual science, but which humans reject or don't even notice. And humans behave towards these beings like cosmic louts.† What kind of beings are they?

* See Rudolf Steiner, *Materialism and the Task of Anthroposophy,* Rudolf Steiner Press, London & Anthroposophic Press, New York 1987. Lecture of May 13, 1921, p. 263f.

† See *Materialism and the Task of Anthroposophy,* p. 261.

The High One: The innermost planet is Vulcan. It's so close to the sun you can't observe it. Beings live on this planet who are now beginning to devote their attention to the earth. Vulcan is the further developed and future form of ancient Saturn, the first stage of the planetary evolution of the earth. And the beings whose sphere of activity is on this planet, are at present almost completely overlooked by humans. Putting it into a picture — they're ready, want to say something to humans but humans shove them around. It's as though you were to continually run around your teacher. Human blindness is still too deep.

WW: What do these beings want to teach humans?

The High One: They want to teach humans the future. They want to teach humans mastery of the spirit self.

WW: Thank you very much for the conversation.

The High One: You're welcome.

37. Kapuvu, the Stone One

Wolfgang Weirauch: Kapuvu, you live permanently. Do you know what development is?

The Stone One: Unfortunately I must have had known it. Otherwise I couldn't have had spoken with humans. Humans only function through their development.

WW: But you yourself don't experience any development?

The Stone One: Yes and no. I am matter. Matter would like to have been developed. I can experience development when humans will have been bringing it to me. Furthermore I will have been formed by the creator forces of the earth and will be all the time. The earth lives.

WW: What are your views on the possibility of individual human development? Would you also like to be able to develop yourself like humans can?

The Stone One: Then I would have to have been dead. I could have had it then. Would you like to have had death as death?

WW: Not at the moment.

The Stone One: Then you understand my problem.

WW: Thank you.

The Stone One: You're welcome. I'd like to have asked something of you. Just think a bit longer about death so that you will have had understood the future of the earth better. In my eyes you humans have been damned to kill death.

WW: How?

The Stone One: When you will have had dissolved matter.

WW: Death is then defeated?

The Stone One: Death is then dead.

WW: And that's a problem for you?

The Stone One: Then I am no more.

WW: Through humans transforming matter into a higher state, won't you similarly be transformed into a higher being?

The Stone One: Then I'm not me.

WW: But a further development of you.

The Stone One: I can't have had known that yet. I'll never be able to have known that.

WW: But probably that's the way it'll be and then you'll re-experience yourself on a higher level.

The Stone One: This hope lights up the earth. Remember that, O human! With Christ!

My Abilities in Spiritual Perception

Verena Staël von Holstein

I can perceive spiritual beings in my surroundings. It takes some time until I come into direct contact with them. The length of time is dependent upon the readiness of the spirit-being to communicate with me, the place where I am and my psychological and physical condition. If I'm in a bad mood, then it's much harder for me to come into contact with an unfamiliar spirit-being. This isn't the case with the spirit-beings familiar to me, with whom I'm constantly in contact.

I can communicate with higher spirit beings of either an elemental or non-elemental kind, when they are willing.

I can perceive the human aura, as well as certain areas of the astral plane. I can infer from the pictures of the etheric body of people, their physical condition and — by comparison with the known basic human types — their character and current emotional state.

I can see the aura of plants and animals. I can speak with the guardian beings of plants and animals, in as much as they're interested.

I can call beings familiar to me and if it's possible they will also appear and I receive a response.

I can perceive the latent energy of things. Sometimes it is given spontaneously to me, at other times I very, very slowly get to see it. This is energy-robbing and tiresome. This is my latest ability.

I can perceive how long some things will last. This is awful and very inhuman.

I can after many years of practice, switch these abilities on and off.

I cannot see over distances. However, images from other spirit beings can be sent to me through familiar spirit beings. These I then have to interpret. This is very prone to error, as the ideas and pictures of spirit beings differ very greatly from those of humans. Spirit beings are also just as different as people. So their statements differ just like those of people.

I can neither perceive the karma of other people nor my own. I wouldn't like that either. I also have no knowledge about my past lives.

I cannot perceive the duration of a person's life.

I cannot read out of the Akashic Chronicle.

I cannot force a spirit being to do something against its will.

Learning to open yourself to nature

Friedrich Pfannenschmidt interviewed by Wolfgang Weirauch

Wolfgang Weirauch: Did you also have contact as a boy to elemental beings?

Friedrich Pfannenschmidt: Not consciously. Unconsciously I must have had contact to them, because my father was a born farmer and practiced his profession with heart and soul. He possessed the ability to be for hours silently at one with himself in nature. And as he often had me with him I've inherited this ability from him.

He probably communicated in an unconscious way with nature spirits, not with his head, but with his feelings. He made many of his decisions after allowing himself such peaceful moments in nature. And this way of communicating I've also inherited from him.

WW: What did you and your father sense when you communicated in this more unconscious way with nature or nature-beings?

FP: From my father I learned to stand on the bridge for hours gazing into the river. By this form of contemplation you open yourself to nature and in doing so we were listening unconsciously and consciously as well, with all our available senses. But you don't just listen, but take in the gestures of nature with all your senses, whether they be colours, smells or sounds. The visual impressions are not even so important. The human being is normally centred on the sense of sight and visual impressions mask out all other sensory impressions. When I communicate with nature in this way, I have to consciously damp down the visual stimuli.

Friedrich Pfannenschmidt

WW: How was it for you as a child and young person living here in the watermill surrounded by nature?

FP: I couldn't imagine it any other way. In later years, it's true, I also travelled around, but I never had the urge to live anywhere else but here. I remember when we were visiting relatives in town, I was quite worn out in the evening, because I could hardly bear the sensations and the large crowds of people in town. That too, hasn't changed to this day. As far back as my memory goes, living together with nature has been the most important thing in my life. More important to me than communicating with people. I avoid people more.

WW: When you got to know your wife, what changes took place in your attitude to nature and especially to the nature-beings?

FP: What I'd previously experienced in a more unconscious way, and couldn't have put into words, all of a sudden I could name with the help of my wife. I have learned to speak about nature-beings. I have learned to find words and expressions for the nature-beings and their work. Through my wife I became acquainted with Anthroposophy and came into conscious contact with Christianity; both weren't part of life at home. And all of a sudden I could give names to my impressions, feelings and perceptions of nature and could begin to think more intensively about them. Before I could only feel — feel at ease or feel uneasy.

WW: When you were able to give names and apply terms to your emotional impressions, was this for you like waking up out of a kind of dream?

FP: Normally a very short moment is associated with the idea of waking-up. In my case, though, this period of time wasn't that short, as it stretched over one or two years. Initially I also rejected quite a few things. It was comfortable to feel, and when someone is suddenly forced to think about things, then it can become a burden. Therefore it wasn't a waking up, more a kind of training.

WW: How has your contact to the nature-beings changed in recent years? How do you sense their presence, when, for example, you're sitting by the river, having to finish something in the garden or repairing something in the house? How do you sense that you're doing something correctly or falsely in terms of the nature-beings?

FP: If I'm planning any changes or renovations to the property — this refers less to ongoing work — then I describe out loud to myself in general terms the planning for my projects, or I get my wife involved. If I neglect this, and work on without caring — without caring in relation to the spiritual aspects, not to the physical aspects — then it can happen that I don't get to finish a job because obstacles build up.

At the moment I'm in the process of repairing the upper floor of the mill. I discuss all jobs, mostly together with my wife, with Miller, the house spirit who's responsible. I explain my plans to him. The basic outline has been clear for a long time, but there are the odd questions of how to do things, in which he has a completely different opinion to mine and over which we often also quarrel with one another a bit, because his ideas cost me more in terms of work and partly also in terms of material. We then have to try and find a compromise.

Miller is the house. And when there are problems with the structure, then I have to ask him, otherwise what I do will make little sense. Sometimes I ignore what Miller wants, and then it can happen that I have twice the work.

WW: Because something's gone wrong?

FP: Because it didn't turn out how I wanted, or because it didn't go how I wanted, or because despite looking five times at a board, I still screwed it on facing the wrong way. Such things happen. Someone puts a spanner in the works. And then you have to have a rethink. It's only common sense to cooperate with the nature-beings.

WW: Do you speak with the other corresponding beings when you do something with the animals, regulate something by the river or carry out changes in the marsh?

FP: Yes. In the case of the animals we have to rely especially on the help of the spirit beings if the animals aren't feeling well. In this wet summer we had problems with the hooves of a few of the sheep. Normally the hoof of a sheep gets worn down by itself, which is also why they're always growing. But in this year with the ground being wet and soft they couldn't wear down. Then the hooves grow too fast, the outer side grows inwards and the sheep start to limp, because dirt collects in the hooves. In such cases, we speak with the spirit beings concerned, with the Brown Ones, if it's reasonable to keep the sheep for about a week in the barn, in order to get them on dry straw so that their hooves can become firm after they've been cut. We also ask if the sheep suffer from standing in the barn, as it's not the time for them to be inside.

WW: Which tasks did you take on for the book project?

FP: I took on the role of the reader. My wife used a dictation programme, and I checked and edited the daily transcriptions. I also read them aloud to myself and tried to understand what the text conveyed. The contents were sometimes ambiguous, and then with the eyes of an outside reader I tried to render the respective accounts more understandable. To some extent I had to really struggle to find the right terms for profound connections. In respect of the spirit, language is sometimes very inflexible. It was therefore my job to give the conversations with the nature spirits style and form.

WW: How was it for you when the nature-beings began to ask you questions?

FP: That was for me a big challenge. Once a week, on Saturday, my wife didn't use the dictation programme, instead I typed directly into the computer. And one Saturday, while we were at work again, the query suddenly came from the Brown One if he might be allowed to question me personally.

At first I had a few misgivings, for no one is so pure in the face of the spiritual world that he can let himself be questioned about everything without second thoughts, without inwardly getting into difficulties. I asked in return what kind of questions they would be and how far they would encroach upon my personal sphere. But I was then assured no questions would be asked either concerning my personality, or affecting my personal freedom or calling it into question.

So then the questions came and each week a different nature-being asked a question. They were mostly quite elementary questions and at the same time quite awakening, so that I was thinking why I'd never asked myself these questions. As a rule they were questions which held a mirror up to humans. The more these questions were asked, the more demanding and challenging I found the whole affair. The questions were always asked on Sundays, I then carried them around with me for a week, and on Saturday answered them. That gave me a lot of pleasure.

WW: I've read the answers to the questions and find that you've answered them well. They were mostly questions which seemed very simple at first sight, but then really demanded quite a lot in order to answer them in detail. I'm thinking, for example, about the question from the Watery One of what the difference is between still water and carbonated water. These are questions that are normally not asked. You've answered the questions in a very pictorial way but nonetheless always got to the core.

FP: That wasn't easy either, and I carried every question around with me for a week. Of course I wasn't thinking about them every minute, but in quiet moments — and I always have some, I make sure of that — I mulled them over.

WW: Did the beings carry on asking questions after the completion of your book project?

FP: It stopped with the completion of the project. At first we were also glad that it was over, as it was very exhausting. But I can well imagine that it'll begin again sometime. I would also be perfectly willing to do it. Now and again there were also questions on the part of the elemental beings.

WW: Do you know whether the beings were satisfied with your answers?

FP: For the most part they were satisfied with my answers, though they weren't often satisfied with the people I had to tell them about. Time and again I had to tell them about the customs and quirks of present-day people, which they didn't like. I especially remember the conversation with the Stone One about the growing practice of laying on of semi-precious stones and their supposed healing effect, which the Stone One considers very questionable.

WW: What task do you take on when your wife speaks with the High One?

FP: I have a moderating effect on her and see myself as someone who's as solid as a rock. Because of my physical build I am, thank God, a very healthy person, and also very connected to the earth, and don't have conscious access to the spiritual world like my wife. When my wife speaks with the High One, I'm a source of calm for her. I hold her hand or touch her on the shoulder. So providing her with a kind of support, both physical and emotional. Indeed it's also happened that I've asked the High One to break off, because my wife was beginning to lose too much control emotionally.

WW: During the twelve Holy Days and the thirteen Holy Nights you took over all the conversations. How did that come about?

FP: That came about through an agreement with the nature-beings, and that was a wonderful experience for me. It was also a very concentrated spiritual atmosphere and until now I haven't come away with so much from any Christian Community service as I have from these conversations at Christmas.

WW: Could you describe in general how you see your position as a connecting link between humans and nature, between humans and the nature-beings?

FP: I'm the one who picks my wife up when she's become too weak, and who also pulls her down when she starts to float away. Both have happened. I try to apply the cooperation with the nature-beings to practical life, because that's something I consider to be urgently necessary. Because the elemental beings, the house spirits and guardian spirits don't want to be worshipped, instead they want their concerns to be respected. They would like to be involved in the activities of humans, they would like to give advice to humans, because they no longer know about many things. Above all they themselves would like human beings to experience them, and the prerequisite is that people know that nature spirits exist. And I see it as my task to bring the contact with the spirit beings, so to speak down from the altar and carry it into everyday life around the kitchen table.

WW: Can you speak about this with other people?

FP: If I'm asked, I answer. There are a few people with whom I can speak about it. Others ask me questions, but basically don't want any answers. Others again don't ask me anything and probably think I'm a bit mad. Or they avoid me, because they consider the whole matter suspicious.

But I also don't want contact to many people at all. People are generally a great strain for me, especially large groups of people. I also perceive the mood in a group of people very directly, and that's sometimes extremely unpleasant. Sometimes I even get attacks of sweating, headaches and stomach aches. This especially occurs when an atmosphere of untruth exists in a group of people. When a person in a group expresses something honest and from the heart, then I experience that on the other hand as pleasant. But then when someone stands up who is more concerned with his own advantage or vanity or is obviously telling an untruth, then my mood switches very quickly and I have to force myself not to walk out.

WW: What have you learned personally through contact with the nature spirits?

FP: I have in the meantime a much greater respect for the Creation. Humility has grown from an unconscious into a conscious ability.

WW: Do you see any further tasks for you in the future?

FP: I would like to assist my children in achieving a responsible interaction with their fellow humans and with the earth, based on their personal freedom. I would like to make it possible for them to have just as beautiful a childhood in this place as I had. Incidentally we all have to make our contribution to the development of humanity.

WW: When now individual readers would like to start making contact with nature-beings, what can you advise them to do and what not to do?

FP: Whoever seeks contact, should not want it. You can't force anything. The classical way of initiation is also associated with many physical and spiritual pains. You have to learn to open yourself to nature. And that by itself is a problem for many people. Many of them are afraid some sort of being will learn too much about them. You have to try and deal with this fear from the very beginning. I had it as well for a time. Who likes to divulge the dark side of his being? When the beings are allowed they gradually become aware of everything about you. You can't fight against this at all. But as I said before, the beings don't want to be worshipped, they want instead, together with humans, to do something good for the earth.

Thematic index